THAT EAGER ZEST

That Eager Zest

FIRST DISCOVERIES IN THE MAGIC WORLD OF BOOKS

AN ANTHOLOGY

SELECTED BY *Frances Walsh*

J. B. LIPPINCOTT COMPANY
PHILADELPHIA AND NEW YORK

Library of Congress Catalog Card Number: 61-12243

42107

November, 1961

ACKNOWLEDGMENTS

The editor and publisher wish to express their appreciation for permission given them to reprint the following:

"New Worlds": from *Memoirs*, by Sherwood Anderson. Copyright 1942 by Eleanor Anderson. Used by permission of Harold Ober Associates, Inc.

"The Vision Then and Now," by Paul Darcy Boles, from *The Living Novel*, ed. Granville Hicks. © 1957 by The Macmillan Company and used with their permission.

"High, Wide and Lonesome": from *High, Wide and Lonesome*, by Hal Borland. Copyright 1956 by Hal Borland. Published by J. B. Lippincott Company.

"Recipe for a Magic Childhood," by Mary Ellen Chase, which first appeared as an article in the May issue of the *Ladies' Home Journal*. Copyright 1951 by The Curtis Publishing Company. Used with permission of The Macmillan Company.

"The Logic of Elfland": from *Orthodoxy*, by G. K. Chesterton. Copyright 1908 by Dodd, Mead & Company. Copyright 1935 by G. K. Chesterton. Reprinted by permission of Dodd, Mead & Company.

"A Plea for Old Cap Collier": from *Irvin S. Cobb at His Best*, by Irvin S. Cobb. Used by permission of Laura Baker Cobb, widow of Irvin S. Cobb, % Buhler, King & Buhler, attorneys, 274 Madison Avenue, New York, N.Y.

"Lost Paradise": from *Lost Paradise*, by Robert P. Tristram Coffin. Copyright 1934 by The Macmillan Company and used with their permission.

"Ever Memorable Day": from *i: Six Nonlectures*, by e. e. cummings. Cambridge, Mass.: Harvard University Press, Copyright 1953 by E. E. Cummings. Reprinted by permission of the publishers.

"All Things Lovely": from *Ringing the Changes*, by Mazo de la Roche. Copyright © 1957 by Mazo de la Roche. Used by permission of Little, Brown & Co.

"Book into Boy": from *Longer Flight*, by Annis Duff. Copyright 1955 by Annis Duff. Quotation from *Bequest of Wings*, by Annis Duff. Both reprinted by permission of The Viking Press, Inc.

"Rapunzel! Rapunzel!" by Carolyn Ellis, originally published in *Good Housekeeping*. Used by permission of the author.

"Book and Child: Three Sonnets," by Paul Engle. Reprinted from *The New York Times Book Review*. Used by permission of the author.

5

The editor wishes to record here warm thanks to John E. Brewton, whose enthusiasm and expert guidance make any experience in the world of children and books a complete delight.

To Nana and Susan

. . . that eager, childlike zest, once caught, is seldom lost. There is no essential difference, for example, between Coleridge's absorption in the "Arabian Nights," and the irrepressible gusto with which John Keats read Shakespeare.

John Livingston Lowes, *Of Reading Books*

FOREWORD

Like a refrain throughout the autobiographical selections on childhood reading experiences collected in this volume is the merry bubble and joy of children meeting the right books—the books for *them*. "I wandered into Paradise by a kind of accident," writes H. L. Mencken. "If I undertook to tell you the effect it had upon me my talk would sound frantic, and even delirious." Hal Borland finds his book on a cheerless Christmas Eve on the plains of Colorado: "I had found something that would shape my whole life." Graham Greene recalls the day he took his fate from the nursery shelves, e. e. cummings the day he knew he would write poetry. The stories that won for Eleanor Farjeon the first international award for the most distinguished children's book were born, she tells us, of the dust of the little bookroom of her childhood.

Childhood is "wrapped clean out of itself" with delight, uncritical in its zest. But the quality of the experience remains, above and far beyond the books and the words themselves. Robert P. Tristram Coffin tells how as a little boy he listened to his father's voice saying Shakespeare to him, long before he knew what half the words were about: "Peter knew from the first, though, that they were about something fine. . . . They came up from something deep. That is the way Peter dreamed the world was going to be, strange and deep and sad, yet like a kind of music."

This eagerness of the young child to stand on tiptoe, to reach beyond himself, leads him at last to the wonderful day of dis-

9

covery: "I tell you I suddenly *read* it, Mummy! I read it all by myself!" So a key turns in a lock, and lands of pleasure lie revealed.

One thinks of Mole in Kenneth Grahame's *Wind in the Willows,* moved by imperious promise in the spring air, suddenly throwing down his broom ("Hang spring housecleaning!") and bolting for the freedom of the friendly meadow, the wide river, and the wild wood beyond. Do you remember the discovery that awaited him there, as he and Ratty rowed along the now familiar river? There came a Piper at the Gates of Dawn:

> "O, Mole! the beauty of it! The merry bubble and joy, the thin, clear happy call of the distant piping! Such music I never dreamed of, and the call in it is stronger even than the music is sweet! Row on, Mole, row! For the music and the call must be for us!"

That eager zest once caught, there comes that period of insatiable, all-out reading, recorded in the last section, when young readers dig, as Robert Louis Stevenson says in his charming "A Gossip on Romance," "like pigs for truffles," knowing what they want and knowing with the wisdom that grows only from delight what reading really is. One wishes for every child so happy a beginning to a lifetime pleasure in books.

Nashville, Tennessee   FRANCES WALSH

CONTENTS

Great Big Wonderful Words

Recipe for a Magic Childhood

Story-sticks and Cobwebs Gold

CONTENTS

One Ever Memorable Day

The Logic of Elfland

CONTENTS

One Day You Met Them

A Sweet Devouring

Great Big

Wonderful Words

Examine the bookcase of a literate moppet and compare it to the tidy shelves of the grown-up's, where dust accumulates and words decay. There sit the childish volumes, dog-eared, ragged of binding, finger-marked and beloved. They have not only been read, they have been fondled, taken to bed, learned by heart. It is a tribute irresistible to the vanity of any author.

—Phyllis McGinley

LEROY F. JACKSON

I've Got a New Book from My Grandfather Hyde

I've got a new book from my Grandfather Hyde.
It's skin on the cover and paper inside,
And reads about Arabs and horses and slaves,
And tells how the Caliph of Bagdad behaves.
I'd not take a goat and a dollar beside
For the book that I got from my Grandfather Hyde.

JOHN McNULTY

Storyteller, Age Three and a Half

"Once upon a time there was a good boy and a bad
boy. . . . But first about the bad boy."

Our son Johnny, now loping
along nicely to the age of three and a half, is our only child, and
as such he is correcting some false ideas I picked up long before
he was born about what children do.

For example, I had thought that three-and-a-halfs were always
asking their fathers to tell them a story. Not this little gent,
Johnny. He works it the other way around. He has employed
various ruses, such as the "I-want-some-milk" ruse, and the "My-
toys-fell-out-of-my-bed" ruse, in order to lure me into his room
half an hour after he has gone to bed and is supposed to be sleeping. Lately, though, he has hit a new device for this purpose. Instead of pleading, with loud hollers, for me to come in and tell
him a story, he shouts, "Please come in here. I want to tell you a
story."

I admit I cannot help falling for this trick, because my curiosity
compels me to wonder what the story will be. So I go in, switch
on the night light before I sit in a chair beside his bed, and tell
him, "Go ahead. You said you'd tell me a story, so go ahead."

Now, what I have come to observe after many repetitions of
this scene is that he seems to have a scheme to embody in these

stories a lot of the personal admirations and, by the same token, the dislikes that are milling in his mind. I know this, because every night the stories take the same form. He says (and I will leave out the mispronunciations), "Once upon a time there was a good boy and a bad boy." That's the unfailing beginning of Johnny's story. Then he says, and he says it very hurriedly, "But first about the bad boy."

That's the giveaway. That's the tip-off, which I recognized only after hearing these stories half a dozen times.

"First about the bad boy," he says, eager to tell about this bad boy he has created—or perhaps remembered from the day's events.

Johnny's story goes on: "Once upon a time there was a bad boy. And do you know what he did? He hit his mommy's typewriter, and he put his hands in the typewriter, and he got his hands all black. Oh, he was a very bad boy!"

I regret to say that at this point there is a look of glee on Johnny's face. It takes no child psychologist to see that although he condemns the actions of the bad boy, this small scoundrel of mine has a tremendous secret admiration for him. His laughing eyes reveal that all too plainly.

"And do you know what else he did?" the story goes on, in Johnny's words. "The bad boy saw his daddy reading the paper in the big chair, and the bad boy went over, and he made a great big hole in the paper his daddy was reading. Oh, he was a very bad boy!"

"Terrible!" I interject, rather hopelessly trying to work in some propaganda against this type of miscreant, the bad boy. "I don't like bad boys. I don't like bad boys at all."

"Oh, no," says Johnny. "We hate bad boys, don't we? We hate bad boys." His words are words of disapproval; but, alas, his ill-concealed laughter betokens deep admiration and more than a little envy of so dashing a personage.

"Not exactly hate them, because we don't hate anybody," I say, in another attempt at propaganda. "We don't like bad boys, that's all. Don't like them at all."

"No, no, we hate bad boys, don't we?" says Johnny, giving the antihate propaganda the fast brush-off. "Do you know what else the bad boy did? Well, when he was coming home from the park, they wouldn't buy him any candy or toys at the store, and the bad boy cried and he sat down on the sidewalk and he wouldn't get up, and when they tried to lift him up, he wouldn't put his feet down, and he sat on the sidewalk and everybody said to his mommy, 'That's a very, very, very bad boy.' That's what the bad boy did. Wasn't he terrible?"

"He'll never get any candy or toys that way," says poor old well-meaning me. "Only good boys get candy; bad boys don't get any candy."

"Oh, no, no, bad boys don't get any candy; only good boys get any candy," Johnny says. "Have you got any Life-Savers, Daddy?"

"Too late for candy," I say. "Time to go to sleep. But now tell me about the good boy. You said you were going to tell me a story about a good boy and a bad boy."

Again I regret to have to say what happens. At mention of the good boy, the admiring, almost idolatrous smile that accompanies the tales of the bad boy vanishes, and Johnny's face becomes downright listless. He pauses a moment, then says in a monotonous rush, "Once-upon-a-time-there-was-a-good-boy-and-he-did-everything-his-mommy-and-his-daddy-told-him BUT FIRST ABOUT THE BAD BOY! Do you know what else he did? Once upon a time there was a bad boy, and he found his daddy's hammer, and he hammered on the floor hard and hard and hard, and everybody got awake downstairs because it was too early, and the bad boy made a very loud noise with the hammer. That's what the bad boy did!"

Again Johnny's eyes are agleam, where with the all-too-brief dismissal of the good boy his eyes were lackluster and even bored. Can it be that the untrammeled, devil-may-care bad boy is his idol, and the conventional little good boy a dreadfully tiresome guy? It looks that way to me.

OGDEN NASH

Rainy Day

Linell is clad in a gown of green,
She walks in state like a fairy queen.
Her train is tucked in a winsome bunch
Directly behind her royal lunch.
With a dignified skip and a haughty hop
Her golden slippers go clippety-clop.
I think I am Ozma, says Linell.
I'm Ozma too, says Isabel.

Linell has discovered a filmy veil;
The very thing for a swishy tail.
The waves wash over the nursery floor
And break on the rug with a rumbling roar;
The swishy tail gives a swishy swish;
She's off and away like a frightened fish.
Now I'm a mermaid, says Linell.
I'm mermaid too, says Isabel.

Her trousers are blue, her hair is kinky,
Her jacket is red and her skin is inky.
She is hiding behind a green umbrella;
She couldn't be Alice, or Cinderella,
Or Puss in Boots, or the Fiddlers Three;
Goodness gracious, who *can* she be?

I'm Little Black Sambo, says Linell.
I'm Sambo too, says Isabel.

Clack the shutters. The blinds are drawn.
Click the switch, and the lights are gone.
Linell is under the blankets deep,
Murmuring down the hill to sleep.
Oh, deep in the soft and gentle dark
She stirs and chirps like a drowsy lark.
I love you, Mummy, says Linell.
Love Mummy too, says Isabel.

MARGARET LEE RUNBECK

How Does "But" Look?

"But I can read," she told them impatiently when
they brought up the subject in school. "I could read
when I was only six inches tall."

AT LAST they've got the idea
across to her. Until she went to school a few weeks ago, she could
read unhampered. She could read whole magazines, page after
page, upside down or right-side up, it didn't matter.

She could read the hieroglyphics scrawled across tree trunks
by growing; she could read sentences the wind scribbled in her
sandbox, and the sepia symbols on the yellow sheet of rice pud-
ding when Lilliam took it out of the oven.

She could read her own nimble scribbling. And I could read
that, too, and sometimes we would sit all morning, I doing my
writing and she doing hers, and we were enchanted and enam-
oured with the amazing things that came out.

Most of all she loved having me read her writing to her, and
she would say, "Did *I* say that?" with such incredulous pride
that I knew that for her at least, I am a poet and a raconteur
without equal.

But now she is six, and the slower, surer ways of education are
to be grappled with.

"But I can read," she told them impatiently when they brought up the subject in school. "I could read when I was only six inches tall."

Now she understands and is chastened at last and almost reconciled to the slower pedantry. Her patient little voice bumps along over the monosyllables as though they were cobblestones.

"Run, Jip, run," she reads obediently. "Jump, Tom, jump." Then she looks up at me and says regretfully, "I *did* so enjoy my own reading. I mean my used-to reading."

I try to explain the advantages of our accepted method, and she listens politely, and I know she is trying to make one more sacrifice for this clumsy logical world which we are asking her to accept in exchange for her slippery, shiny, delicious, private one.

But they have got the idea across to her at last. She came home and explained it to me.

"You see, everything has a shape. All the words," she said, "they're little pictures of themselves. They don't look like themselves, but anyhow you get so you know them when you see them." . . .

Once she learned the idea, it became a little stamp without which nothing was valid. She had to try it on everything. She kept asking me to show her how Tree looks, and how Wagon, and we write the words, and we make a crude sketch beside it, for that is the newest method of association.

But yesterday we got into trouble with her logicalness. . . .

"How does But look?" she asked the teacher. "I'd like to see a picture of But, please."

The other children, always prepared for the onslaught of knowledge, sat quietly waiting to see But drawn on the blackboard.

"Well . . . these are the letters," Miss Grover said, writing them in the stiff-legged printing they know at six.

"But how does it *look?*" she insisted. "I'd like to see its picture."

"Well . . . it doesn't look like anything," Miss Grover said helplessly.

"But it must look like something," Boo said. "Everything looks like something."

Miss Grover is a resourceful teacher. When all authority fails, she turns her pupils back upon themselves. It's something they might as well learn at six, for in the larger pantograph, they'll find it happening to them many times.

"Well, if you think it looks like something, you may draw it, dear."

Boo tried all afternoon, and still it wasn't quite right. She knew; you could see that. It was only her fingers that were inarticulate. But at last she got it, and it was so satisfactory to her that she didn't even need to show it for confirmation. She folded up the paper and put it in her pocket and brought it home.

"*You* know how But looks, don't you?" she said to me while we were taking off her rubbers.

"Vaguely," I said.

"Well, this is the way it looks to me." She unfolded the paper, and there were two bean-shaped objects, facing each other and joined, as though one might be regarding the other in a mirror. But one was green and one was red.

"*But* is two," she explained, her wide eyes pleading that I agree. "They look alike but they're opposite."

I saw exactly what she meant. Similar, and yet, on the contrary, not at all. I knew exactly what she was trying to show, because I have been confounded by butness all my life. The simplest thought always bringing with itself its shadowy other-shape, alike and oppositely colored.

The minor butness that echoes from joy; the almost silent flute-notes above even sorrow.

ROBERT GRAVES

The Poet in the Nursery

The book was full of funny muddling mazes,
  Each rounded off into a lovely song,
And most extraordinary and monstrous phrases
  Knotted with rhymes like a slave-driver's thong,
And metre twisting like a chain of daisies
  With great big splendid words a sentence long.

I took the book to bed with me and gloated,
  Learning the lines that seemed to sound most grand;
So soon the pretty emerald green was coated
  With jam and greasy marks from my hot hand,
While round the nursery for long months there floated
  Wonderful words no one could understand.

ANNIS DUFF

Book into Boy

"I tell you I suddenly *read* it, Mummy! I read it all by myself!"

OUR son discovered one day when he was about five years old that he could read—and came hurtling bumpity-bumpity-bump all the way down the stairs in his eagerness to tell me about it. He picked himself up, still clutching a book under his arm, gabbling in such a dither of excitement that I wondered momentarily if a bang on the head had loosened something vital. When he paused for breath I asked him if he had damaged himself. He looked at me blankly.

"*Damaged* myself? I should think not! I tell you I suddenly *read* it, Mummy! I read it all by myself! I read *The Little House!*"

Here was cause for rejoicing, to be sure, but little for surprise. We had known for a long time, from his diminishing satisfaction with an hour or two a day of being read aloud to, and his increasing impatience to "get at the *insides* of books for myself," that he felt a need—deep and strong and *right*—to learn to read. Now, all at once, he realized that he had made a beginning at satisfying that need, and his happiness was beautiful to behold.

But the real beginning, as we knew, had been made already; at the age of two he was a confirmed book-lover, and three of the

28

books that he never tired of looking at and listening to when he was a tiny boy remained in his mind as the foundation of his five-year-old success in finding out for himself "what the words say" on a printed page. As our daughter had pointed out to us when she was learning to read, a word is, after all, "just a little chain of letters," and letters are delightful things to a child who meets them in Walter Crane's *Absurd ABC,* Kate Greenaway's *A Apple Pie,* and C. B. Falls' superb *ABC Book.* Beautiful drawing and lovely colors please the eyes; amusing words tickle the fancy and associate themselves happily with sounds of letters that are fun to play with.

Our daughter's pleasure in these books led her, at the age of four, to invent a game to amuse her father. "Draw me a picture of 'bĕ,'" she would say, and he would make a handsome big B and a swarm of little bs flying around a hive. Then she would demand "one for me to guess," and a small, fierce lion might appear on the paper, growling in large R-R-Rs, or a grinning boy with a bowl of cherries, saying M-M-M! This game she taught to her brother, who very soon outgrew the need to have anyone draw letters, because he found them for himself all over the place. "M-E-N," he would spell out in a stentorian voice in a railway station; "I-N" at the entrance to a one-way street. S-t-o-p, g-o, g-a-s, e-x-i-t, were frequently met combinations of letters that he soon learned to recognize as words.

One day we were crossing a fortunately not too busy intersection where the word SLOW had been newly painted in enormous yellow letters on the road. "Don't tell me what it is," he cautioned. "Let me read it for myself!" And with insouciant deliberation he went for a walk, along the curves of the S, sharp left turn on the L, "round about and round about" on the O, and a careful zigzag on the W. Then he stood for what seemed like a full half-hour where he could look at the letters "upside-up." At last,

"That word says 'slow,'" he remarked calmly, and we continued on our way.

Any boy who takes in "chains of letters" through eyes and ears and the very soles of his feet will be a real reader, and our son certainly is that. From the momentous day when he took possession of *The Little House* for himself he has assimilated books with such rapturous response that we long ago parodied Walter de la Mare's

> Whatever Miss T. eats
> Turns into Miss T.

to fit our conviction that

> Whatever Mr. D. reads
> Turns into Mr. D. . . .

PHYLLIS McGINLEY

Plea in a Children's Bookshop

Do you have a book for a literate girl
   Who's six years old tomorrow?
A book to be read when it's time for bed
   And hidden from those who borrow?
She leans to the magic of just-suppose,
   She's fond of a tale that's merry,
But she doesn't care how the story goes
   Or whether it's true or fairy,
And she doesn't mind how the pictures look.
   She'd blink at a price inflation,
So long as the book is a regular book
   Instead of an Animation.

Sir or Madam, I beg you hop up.
Find her a volume that doesn't pop up,
Fold, make comical noises, bend,
Waggle, or wiggle, or stand on end—
Something not so up-to-the-minute,
That isn't sold with a record in it
Or a chime that rings if your fingers strike it.
It may be Art, but she doesn't like it.

Her eyes would glisten if she might listen
   To Sinbad the Sailor's progress.

With sweet compliance she'd hear of giants,
  Or ogres, or maybe an ogress.
She'd like a dwarf of a proper size
  Or a stepmother cruel and clever.
But she doesn't want them to roll their eyes,
  Propelled by a paper lever.
Away with audible tigers, please,
  And sheep (you can comb their wool out).
The lady's learning her A.B.C.'s
  And she isn't amused by a Pull-out.

Seller of narratives juvenile,
Scan your counter and search your aisle.
Surely somewhere amid the welter
A book immobile is taking shelter
Whose pictured dragon, whose painted wizard
Wasn't designed to be stroked or scissored,
Pasted, colored, or strung with beading.
Haven't you anything meant for *reading?*

By the Boots of Puss, by the Captain's Hook,
I swore to buy her a just plain book,
For novelty stuff is tears and sorrow
When a girl's about to be six tomorrow.

WILLIAM McFEE

Harbours of Memory

"David Copperfield" is for me the great book of my
life. It begins on Page One with the simple and majestic declaration, "I Am Born". . . . I said to myself "I,
too, have been born" and lay flat on my stomach on
the hearthrug to pursue the tale anew.

I⊤ is a harmless diversion of au-
thors to express a weakness for various methods of beginning a
story. Very few eminent authors seem able to resist the distant
horseman of G. P. R. James's novels, who might have been seen
as the shades of night were falling. Blessed with perfect faith and
eyesight one may agree. Others like what used to be called a
Proem, a sort of literary shock absorber, a kind of intermediate
chamber where one is accustomed to a change of atmosphere before being transferred to the full pressure of the story. It was a
favourite device of novelists when I was a youngster, and I re-
garded their Proems with aversion because they had no ascer-
tainable connection with the story. Others were drawn toward the
letter form, the first chapter, or perhaps introduction, ushering the
reader into the very innermost shrines of intimacy. Others again
like to go head-foremost into the very thick of the action. Authors
who do this are practical. They "get" the reader with a short
scene of gun play in a Western camp and tell him what the
trouble was afterward. Shrewd fellows they are!

But personally the one story I cannot resist is the story whose first chapter begins with a birth. "David Copperfield" is for me the great book of my life. It begins on Page One with the simple and majestic declaration,

"I Am Born"

and I began to read it not very long after I had been born myself. Being born, at the time when that fat and fascinating volume first came into the nursery, was about the only thing I had accomplished without mishap. I said to myself "I, too, have been born" and lay flat on my stomach on the hearthrug to pursue the tale anew. There is nothing like a start, and being born, however pessimistic one may become in later years, is undeniably a start. And I defy any one to resist the attractive possibilities of a being who has achieved the momentous feat of getting himself born.

But as time went on and I read "David Copperfield" so many times that whole episodes are graven verbatim on my memory, I began to discover a number of startling divergences between David's conventional arrival in England and my own. David, it seemed, was a posthumous child, a hard word which gave me a lot of trouble in the beginning. Inquiry revealed the agreeable fact that I was not posthumous. No one will ever fathom the extraordinary concrete images evoked in a child's mind by elusive abstractions. For some reason the word posthumous called up ideas of strange convoluted things seen in Doré's illustrations of Dante's Inferno. Further investigations carried on in the family circle elicited the fact that I myself was an exasperating child and a fit candidate for that grim neighbourhood. I was also a child afflicted with innumerable privileges no other child had, none of which seemed to do me any good. Like most English children of the 'eighties' I became reconciled to the fact that I was a bad lot and only some special intervention would save me from an alarming end.

But at that time I was only remotely interested in ends. It was beginnings which preoccupied the infant imagination. In due course it was possible to visualize the differences between Copperfield's beginnings and my own. Copperfield, after getting born in a house in Suffolk, achieved felicity by going to live in a ship. I, on the contrary, had come out of a ship to live in a house. This seemed to me hard luck. . . .

ROBERT HILLYER

Seven Times One Are Seven

In his grandmother's garden was a cake with seven candles,
And the family had forgathered that rose-haunted afternoon.
Aunt Jane was singing Jean Ingelow's verses
About a seventh birthday to a sentimental tune.
"It's a birthday to remember," said his grandmother smiling,
"With all the roses out on the third day of June."

His brother said, "There should have been eight candles. One to
    grow on."
"For seven years," the Rector said, "I think he's pretty tall."
They talked about him amiably as though he were not present,
And he felt at his own party embarrassingly small.
His mother sat in silence, and he knew the scent of roses
Had made her think—as he did—of his father's funeral.

The books for his birthday had all been sent from England.
"No one writes for children like the English," said Aunt Jane.
"How about Louisa May Alcott?" asked the Rector.
"Only fit for girls," said his brother with disdain.
His uncle coughed and murmured, "There's *Huckleberry Finn.*"
"Good heavens!" said his grandmother, "that vulgar Mark
    Twain?"

Momently his birthday was slipping through his fingers,
Till, "Blow and make a wish," said his sister. So he blew.

Out went four candles, the wind blew out the other three,
And he was disappointed that he'd blown out so few.
His mother said, "How wonderful! Four sevenths of your happiness
Is way above the average for your wishes to come true."

The Rector and the members of the older generation
Put aside their plates and settled comfortably to chat.
His brother went to baseball, his sister to a friend's house,
And everything seemed quite commonplace and flat.
Freed from all attention now, his birthday party over with,
He chose a book called *Storyland* and lost himself in that.

CARL SANDBURG

"Where Shall We Go?"

"Here you are, little Queer Stories."

"WHERE shall we go?" was often a question. At the Public Library, on Main near the Square, on the second floor, you heard no talk. At the librarian's desk they whispered like they had secrets. It was as still as in a church when the preacher reads the text. You could cough or sneeze if you had to. You were supposed to read and think. When two of us kids looking at a funny picture happened to snicker out loud, we would find eyes on us. You came to be quiet and learn something.

On reading tables were magazines and the Galesburg and Chicago newspapers. I went through the catalogue back and forth, reading titles of books and trying to guess what was good for me. The catalogue was an eye-opener on how many books and how many different books there are in the world. I wondered if anyone in Galesburg had read all the books in the catalogue and how you could make a catalogue without reading all the books in it.

As soon as I could I wanted to get a card to take out books and they told me I had to make an ap-pli-ca-tion. So I learned how to apply by filling out an ap-pli-ca-tion. I got my card and began taking out books, one by one, and the date I took the book out got stamped on my card. One by one I read all the books in the library by Horatio Alger, Oliver Optic, and C. A. Stephens. When all the books by those authors were out, I tried Hans Christian Andersen, and if he was out then some kind of *Strange Tales* of this and that.

One day in a library book I noticed that the population of the earth in the year I was born was 1,439,029,600. I puzzled over whether they had counted me and how if they hadn't counted me the number should be changed to 1,439,029,601. I was beginning arithmetic and it was fun to add one, which was me, and make a big number so odd you couldn't divide it by two and make it come out even. And when I read in the same book that fifteen million Chinese people had died in a famine that year I was born, I puzzled over whether they had been subtracted from 1,439,029,600.

Miss Phillips, the librarian, was perched on a high stool back of a high desk and I stood tiptoe to hand her my card. She had a prim face, a long straight nose, and eyeglasses. I believed she had read many of the books in the catalogue and was the best-posted woman in Galesburg on books. One afternoon the books I wanted were all out, and I went back to the catalogue and wrote more numbers of books. Only one I wanted was in. It was named *Queer Stories for Children*. As Miss Phillips handed the book toward me and I reached up for it, she said with a smile I didn't like, "Here you are, little Queer Stories." I could have thrown the book in her face, though I didn't. She called me little and I had got over being little. Worse yet, she as much as called me "queer" and if you're queer you act queer, think queer, and talk queer. I said to myself she deserved the long nose she had and I wished it would get longer. And if I was queer she was snippity and I would rather be queer than snippity.

MARGARET SECRIST

Margaret Was Stranger

When summer, all clover cologne,
meandered the meadows of dew,
I made up my ten-year mind
to be a horse, and swiftly pursue
all the bird-sung hours of the hay-sweet day.
I shook my flaxen, braided mane;
I pawed hot dust, and shied to the fence,
mildly amazing the cows in the lane.
I scratched my flanks on blackberry briars
and splashed bare hooves in a stony brook
where mud-lulled crayfish fearfully backed
away from my fierce, blue look.
I pulled the innermost shoot
of sweet flag and ate its bitter heart;
then I cantered the knolls to kneel in a bed
of wild, warm strawberries, sweet and tart.
Lip-stained, I loped through a lake
of sun-daft daisies blown to white caps.
Here I rolled in the waves and lay
watching the surf break sky into scraps.

"Margaret, oh Margaret, where are you?"
my grandmother called suddenly.
But I could never go home again,
for I was Black Beauty asleep in the daisies,
and Margaret was stranger to me!

PAUL HAZARD

The World Republic of Childhood

Yes, children's books keep alive a sense of nationality;
but they also keep alive a sense of humanity . . . each
of them is a messenger that goes beyond mountains
and rivers, beyond the seas, to the very ends of the
world. . . .

WHEN I was a youngster, I re-
member seeing, in my mind's eye, the whole world spread out before me. One fine day I escaped from my dull town, and with
two boys of my own age, André and Julien, traveled all over
France through the pages of a beautiful book: Le tour de la
France par trois enfants. Another time, led by Don Quixote and
Sancho, I saw the plains of Castile, white-hot in the sun, with
dusty roads and inns full of adventure. I knew the cork trees and
the wild thickets of the Sierra Morena. In my imagination I saw
desert isles, the northern lights on the sea. I visited the pigmy
country in Africa, which did not seem strange to me as I was
familiar with Lilliput. I lived in Uncle Tom's Cabin and cultivated sugar cane with black slaves as companions. Like the
Baron Munchausen, I fastened a rope to the crescent moon so I
could glide to earth, and the rope being too short I cut it above me
to attach it to the end which was hanging under my feet. I went
everywhere with Jules Verne, even to the very bottom of the
ocean, and I saw

. . . the greens, the blues,
through which, pale, dreaming,
sometimes a drowned man sinks . . .[1]

Yes, children's books keep alive a sense of nationality; but they also keep alive a sense of humanity. They describe their native land lovingly, but they also describe faraway lands where unknown brothers live. They understand the essential quality of their own race; but each of them is a messenger that goes beyond mountains and rivers, beyond the seas, to the very ends of the world in search of new friendships. Every country gives and every country receives—innumerable are the exchanges—and so it comes about that in our first impressionable years the universal republic of childhood is born. . . .

Smilingly the pleasant books of childhood cross all the frontiers; there is no duty to be paid on inspiration. . . .

[1] Rimbaud, from "Le Bateau ivre," in *Poésies complètes*, 1895.

PAUL ENGLE

Book and Child: Three Sonnets

I

High from these printed, silent sounds, the bird
That carried Sinbad and his diamonds hangs
Out of this cave of frightful phrase and word
Old tiger roars between his ripping fangs.
Down from the grassy hills of this plain prose
Indian horse and warrior surprise,
The boy hears yells of Gall and Roman Nose
And Custer's yellow hair screams in his eyes.

Battle comes to his bedroom. In his fright
His hands jerk back as if the book would bite.
But goes on reading, takes that book to bed,
By all that verbal violence comforted,
Happy to see, in his devoted rage,
The whole world come alive on that dead page.

II

She tries to read, but words are only jumbles
Of shapes that twist her tongue until it clashes:
Long consonants are sticks on which she stumbles,

Round vowels are muddy pools through which she splashes.
Dog is a sound that bristles like a bark,
Cat is a sound that yowls and turns up fur.
But no shape on that page is a real mark
For living animals that play with her.

She throws the book down, her feet start to stamp.
Shocked at her act, she takes it, holds it tight,
Knowing that from these pages, secret, dumb,
Her long-loved story once again will come.
Her eyes fill, not with words, tears, mad, but light.
That book glows in her like a turned-up lamp.

III

Animal stories make the world a zoo
In which the fiercest animal is you.
When the book says, Rain fell and thunder rolled,
They shake, and huddle down against the cold.
But when they turn the page and read, The sun
Came out and all the clouds went, one by one,
They look up toward the light and smile for knowing
They hold the sky in their hands, blue and blowing.

No fierce ghost prowling through its haunted house,
No golden nymph turned greenly into tree,
No mouse changed into monster, back to mouse,
No spook from caves, no demon from the sea,
Has so intense and wild and lost a look
As children holding in their hands a book.

Recipe for a

Magic Childhood

. . . people who take poetry, along with books and music and all beautiful things, as major blessings; and who believe in sharing these things with children as freely and casually as daily bread.

—ANNIS DUFF

MacKINLAY KANTOR

But Look, the Morn

Whenever I hear Horatio speak, I cannot contemplate
the dew on fabled hills of a sixteenth century Denmark. Instead the hills are hard with snow; they are
Iowa hills. . . .

I WOULD hear her voice. Hamlet,
in a February dawn, in an Iowa town of five-thousand-two-
hundred-and-eight, with the brass sun coming up out of trees beyond the Boone River.

"But look, the morn, in russet mantle clad
Walks o'er the dew of yon high eastward hill. . . ."

I have heard Horatio speak that line many times, when the
black garb of Hamlet was put on by Evans or Olivier or Gielgud.
I have seen the king's ghost vanish at cock-crow in New York
and Chicago, in Dublin and London, in Stratford itself. Whenever I hear Horatio speak, I cannot contemplate the dew on fabled
hills of a sixteenth century Denmark. Instead the hills are hard
with snow; they are Iowa hills, with the last tufts of prairie grass
bent beneath their sleet in the cow pastures. The sun creeps higher
to tint the bare branches and chimneys under them.

My mother's voice, charged with willingness to contemplate
the miracle of her dawning day: "So I have heard and do in part
believe. . . . But look, the morn—" . . .

49

LIZETTE WOODWORTH REESE

Bible Stories

The room was low and small and kind;
   And in its cupboard old,
The shells were set out to my mind;
   The cups I loved with rims of gold.

Then, with that good gift which she had,
   My mother showed at will,
David, the ruddy Syrian lad,
   With his few sheep upon a hill.

A shop down a rude country street,
   And chips strewn on the floor,
And faintly keen across the heat;
   The simple kinsfolk at the door.

Mary amid the homely din,
   As slim as violet;
The little Jesus just within
   About His Father's business set.

My mother rose, and then I knew
   As she stood smiling there,
Her gown was of that gentle blue
   Which she had made the Virgin wear.

RECIPE FOR A MAGIC CHILDHOOD

How fair the very chairs were grown!
The gilt rose on each back
Into a Syrian rose was blown,
And not our humble gold and black.

That week long, in our acres old,
Lad David did I see;
From out our cups with rims of gold,
The little Jesus supped with me.

DOROTHY WHITE

Reading Before Five

She has always liked to peer at the shoe lost amongst
the cabbages but . . . "Where is the shoe among the
potatoes? Where are the potatoes?"

30 December 1948

THIS morning was a true mid-
summer day. Ann and Carol were soon overtired with running
about and I suggested stories under the trees. Ann asked for
Peter Rabbit, which they have been reading about once a fortnight for a long time now. My impression is that they ask different questions every time I read the book and find something new
there, much as I find something new every time I pick up *Emma*
or *Middlemarch.* The children's classic seems to propagate itself
like a bulb, and because of this and because Beatrix Potter's English is so pleasing, I too never become bored with Peter. Yet there
are other stories that the children obviously enjoy which reduce
me to eternal screaming point by the time I've read them ten or
twelve times.

Today it was the picture of Flopsy, Mopsy, and Cottontail
gathering blackberries which caught their fancy, probably because a few days ago the two of them were over in the section beyond the bush. Together with young Margaret, Carol and Ann
enjoyed the illicit pleasures of picking black-currants meant for

jam. In the story they obviously associated the blackberries with the currants.

Once or twice lately, when I have left the house to go visiting or down to the library or when Dick has left for work in the mornings, Carol has been calling admonishments. I had been a little puzzled because her manner and material have not been a direct imitation of what I or her father would say on like occasions. It has an alien element in it, like an unidentified flavour in a dish for which one thought one knew the recipe. I've just realized that into my normal cautions she had blended Mrs. Rabbit's "You may go into the fields and down the lane but don't go into Mr. McGregor's garden." Yesterday when I left her next door while I went to town she called back after me, "Mummy." Then, holding her head on one side and putting on the half-smiling, half-stern face which signals that she is acting, she said, "Don't go on the street cars, run over and get some buns, and don't go in Mr. McGregor's garden."

Again last week before breakfast, a leisurely Sunday morning being in progress, I found Carol crawling about the hall, a "pretendy" Peter on all fours eating invisible radishes. She bounded over to a sofa (alias toolshed) and asked me to be McGregor. I had to look under the flower pots as he did in the story while from her "watering can" there came a realistic sneeze. That Sunday this game was played on and off all day. . . .

21 *December 1949*

Dick has bought *Little Black Sambo*. Here once again one notices the exquisite use of "and."

And Black Mumbo made him a beautiful little red coat and a pair of little blue trousers. And Black Jumbo went to a bazaar and bought him a beautiful green umbrella and a lovely little pair of purple shoes with crimson soles and crimson linings.

Carol listened to this with real awe, a different response from the easy acceptance of *Davy's Day* and different too from the response to *That Baby,* when all her deepest feelings were involved. Black Sambo represents drama to Carol: after all he is threatened many times with being eaten alive, definitely adventure by any standards. Yet there was no terror as she listened, and I have been wondering why. Is it because the story begins with Little Black Sambo in security? His mother and father are there, solid, before any tigers appear on the scene. After this adventure, the hero is back in security. "And they all sat down to supper. And Black Mumbo ate 27 pancakes, and Black Jumbo ate 55, and Little Black Sambo ate 169 because he was so hungry."

The story is an adventure, not a nightmare. In an adventure the principal character goes forth from security to insecurity and back to port; a nightmare is an adventure without a port. *Paul Alone in the World* by this criterion is nightmare, and so of course are many modern novels. The film, *Dead of Night,* owed much of its terror to precisely this absence of port.

We read the book once four days ago. This morning she came into my bed and said, "I'm Black Sambo and you are the tiger and you say I'm going to eat you all up." So at the crack of dawn we went through the story. She gave me blue trousers and a red coat, prompted me to tie a knot in my tail to carry the green umbrella, but finally became rather muddled by the purple shoes with crimson soles and crimson linings.

"Things have to be imagined to tell," Walter de la Mare says somewhere. Little Black Sambo had told. . . .

26 March 1950

Today as I stood by the stove stirring a sauce Carol said, "Tell me some poems." So I recited as I stirred, *John had great big waterproof boots on, Double double toil and trouble, Dr. Fell, Someone came knocking,* and one or two others, until my memory for "suitable poetry" completely failed. "More," the demanding voice kept saying. So I went on to

> *When as the rye reach to the chin*
> *And chopcherry, chopcherry ripe within*
> *Strawberries swimming in the cream*
> *And schoolboys swimming in the stream,*
> *Then, O, then, O, then, O, my true love said*
> *Till that time come again*
> *She could not live a maid.*

"Chopcherry, chopcherry," Carol chanted. "More!" So I recited *Daffodils* and the *Ode on a Grecian Urn*. "That's a long one. More!" However by now the sauce was done and the rest of the dish required all my thought.

I had the impression as I spoke that Carol would have listened to absolutely anything I said even if it had been poetry in a foreign language. It's as if she does a special kind of listening when you fix your eye on her in ancient-mariner style. Certainly it's a different kind of attention from that which she gives me when I read to her. There is a wide gulf that lies between reciting or telling aloud and reading, like the gulf between reading to one child and reading to fifty. . . .

WALKER GIBSON

Who Reads What to Whom

How all the mysteries of life unfold
At bedtime, reading to a six-year-old,
When tangled knots inscrutable to me
Unravel in the ear of infancy!
Why plumbing really works. What makes cars run.
How any boy can make a rocket gun.
Electric currents. Love among the ants.
What sewage does inside disposal plants.
I never knew, until I read these books,
How igloos are constructed by Chinooks,
And how a kind of tank car carries ink,
And how a cold front moves, and why stones sink.
Surely with all that Useful Information
My boy must be well on toward maturation;
In fact at six he may be past his prime
And might as well take over, any time.

    Well, let him then. And let *him* read to *me*—
But I'll decide what book it's going to be.
Revenge! He'll get no fatherly compassion.
I'll make him read me everything in fashion:
A little Kierkegaard, perhaps, tonight?
Finnegans Wake? Or Gide for something light?

Kafka? The *Cantos? Howl? World Almanac?*
Or shall we try that fellow Kerouac,
In Frisco on the bum from New York City,
Enjoying little pangs of sweet self-pity?

That does it! Even infants can be bored.
"You read now, Daddy. How concrete gets poured.
How to pan gold. Why lizards multiply.
What litmus does when fed on alkali.
How pioneers in jungles make a clearing."
My boy, no more of bedtime engineering.
Now that at last I've got you on a barrel,
It's Edward Lear for you, and Lewis Carroll.
It's Tweedledum and Tweedledee for you—
If you don't like them, never mind. I do.
So while we take a nice old-fashioned stroll
With Alice down that well-worn rabbit hole,
You'll see the point of bedtime literature—
It's to make parents sleep safe and secure.

LIONEL TRILLING

Rearing and Reading

You have arrived at that notable moment which no
one, to my knowledge, has ever celebrated or even remarked, the moment when the child can be read to out
of a real book.

Y‌ou have been reading to your
child for quite a few years now, and you continue to do so even
though the child has overcome, or is beginning to overcome, his
illiteracy. And you have arrived at that notable moment which
no one, to my knowledge, has ever celebrated or even remarked,
the moment when the child can be read to out of a real book.

Up to this point the pleasure of reading aloud has been mixed.
You were of course entranced the first time the child trotted in
with some tall thin volume in his hands and held it out to you
with the terse command, "Read!" It is hard to know just what
satisfactions he expects from your obedience. Perhaps he wishes
only to be hypnotized and stilled by the sound of your voice—
he has perhaps had his first impulse to escape from the burden of
himself. But he has connected that strangely composite object, a
book, with some notion of satisfaction. (Like Gesell, I say *he,*
when I mean *he or she.*) And manifestly he conceives what is not
actually before his eyes, and makes sense of it, and your pleasure
in seeing him do this never abates.

But it is, as I say, a mixed pleasure. The fact is that the child's taste and your taste are but little alike. Not that there is no literature that pleases both the very young child and the adult. The nursery rhymes have enough ambiguity in their meaning, and charm in their tone, to involve us to some degree, possibly to a greater degree than they involve the modern child himself. And you find that you do discriminate among the elaborate picture books, and even among the Little Golden Books, to which you retreat because the others are so very expensive.

Among these books written for the very young child there are some which are charming and gay, free of archness and false sentiment. From them the child seems to derive pleasure and you are at least not pained by them. Indeed, for a while you are rather pleased by your immersion in the world of primary colours and motives. But the number of really good books for the very young child is limited. The chances are about even that any given book will not be fresh and gay but *chic* and affected, false in tone, not really innocent. And you seldom feel that the book is alive, existing by reason of its own necessity to exist. It is likely to be a mere product, the result of the conscious effort of an industry to satisfy a demand, of editorial conferences, of psychological and pedagogical doctrine (*i.e.,* dogma), of university courses which teach how books for children should be contrived.

But you are embarked. You have committed yourself to the practice of reading aloud and there is no turning back. Books have become a part of the child's life. You stick it out. Stories about animals are better, as a rule, than stories about people, and in my experience rabbits are the best of the animals. You endure and wait for the moment when your own interests will be better represented.

That moment comes, it really does come. And it brings more pleasure than you could have guessed. I have never abated my admiration of *The Jungle Books,* however harshly I may have thought of Kipling. But it was not until I read the stories aloud that I fully understood how wonderful they are. I approached them with some hesitation, remembering how much they had meant to me at about the same age as that of my listener. I need not have worried, nothing could have been more successful. "Rikki-Tikki-Tavi" was, to be sure, a mistake; it made trouble in the form of night fears, and it *is* frightening, probably because the snake invades a little boy's house and because the little boy is only incidental to the story, and quite passive—if he and not the mongoose were the hero, there would, I think, have been no trouble. But the adventures of Kotick, the white seal, the culture-hero of his race, were highly relished. As for the great Mowgli stories, they proved a transcendent delight. And now reader and listener were on a parity. "When Akela died I felt as if my stomach fell," said the listener. Yes, that was it exactly, but I had to give my assent in a minimal way because the death of the Lone Wolf, the great old leader of the Seeonee Pack, had been so affecting that (as they used to say in novels) I did not trust myself to speak. . . .

ROBERT LAWSON

The Gawk Eros

When we became too awful, Miss Barrowes would
sigh resignedly, take down a book, and read to us
. . . . as I listened in an ecstatic, sleepy trance, my
mind went at fashioning our future—together.

A s I have said, there were often
great age gaps between us and our true loves. My first, for example, was Miss Barrowes, our teacher. I cannot remember just
what grade it was she taught, I think it was about the fourth, so I
was fairly young, and while she was by no means an ancient
spinster, she must have been my senior by fifteen years or so.
However, this mattered not at all; I adored her. I can't imagine
why, but I think it must have been her voice, for although I have
not the faintest recollection of what she looked like, I can still
remember her low, mellow voice as she read to us.

At that age school was a frightful bore for healthy young animals. We hadn't learned enough to have any real interest in
studies; concentrating on any one thing for more than ten minutes
at a time was terribly exhausting. In winter our shoes were always wet and our chilblains itched and burned. In spring it was
even worse—school ran then until almost the end of June. The
horse-chestnuts blooming outside the open windows, sounds and
smells of spring, lilacs and apple blossoms, wandering bees, flower

hawkers, and the peanut man's whistle all served to reduce us to a squirmy, scratching, unbearable aggregation of young hoodlums. When we became too awful, Miss Barrowes would sigh resignedly, take down a book, and read to us. She read us *The Prince and the Pauper,* which, as she read it, I thought was the grandest book in the world. She gave us parts of *Huckleberry Finn* and reams of poetry.

These were the only moments of school that I didn't hate, and as I listened in an ecstatic, sleepy trance, my mind went at fashioning our future—together. She evidently loved books, I loved books too, all my family did; we had a common bond.

What more natural, then, than that my dreams should form about a lifetime of evenings spent by crackling log fires while we read to each other? I (who had never quite succeeded in mastering the first ten lines of "The Village Blacksmith") would declaim Byron and Shelley, Tennyson and Browning, by the hour (from memory, of course), while she would quietly raise her eyes from some equally worthy book and listen in rapt attention. It was a grand life.

The only way in which I could demonstrate my adoration was by clapping erasers. At that time three sides of the schoolroom were covered by slate blackboards on which a great deal of our work was done. By the end of the day they were a mess, and the felt erasers were thoroughly filled with chalk dust. It was evidently the teacher's duty to see that these were cleaned up; a duty that she accomplished in various ways. Sometimes refractory pupils were kept after school and forced to do it. Sometimes good little girls volunteered for the duty. Oftener than not, I fear, poor Teacher did it herself.

The thought of this dainty and cultured lady of my heart doing such dirty work was unbearable, so I constituted myself chief-volunteer-eraser-clapper. When school was dismissed I dawdled around until Becky and the rest were well away. If there were no volunteers or peon labor present, I made my way to the desk where Miss Barrowes wearily wrote and mumbled, "C'n I—er—may I clap the erasers?" She always assented; who wouldn't? I gathered up a whole scrapbasket of the filthy things and took them down to the yard to clap.

As I happily banged them together the choking clouds of chalk dust were as the smoke of incense rising from the altar of my adoration. Then there were the blackboards to wipe down with a damp rag, fresh chalk to be laid out and the old broken pieces to be gathered up; a delightful few minutes all alone with my idol, who, however, always continued her writing, apparently unconscious of my presence. I am sure now that she was writing to her fiancé, for she was married a few months later, but fortunately I didn't know about that.

Everything finished, I would grab my cap, receive her gracious "Thank you very much, Robert," and gallop home, my heart swollen with happiness at having rendered a loving service. This devotion continued for what seemed the better part of a lifetime (it must have been all of three or four months), until the night she came to dinner.

At that time it was the custom of most of our parents to invite Teacher to dinner once each year. Ordinarily it was a pretty painful occasion all around, but this time I could hardly wait for it and deviled Mother incessantly until the formal note had been dispatched and the date arranged. Our affair being on such a high cultural plane, I was dying to have Miss Barrowes realize how truly aesthetic my background was. I was sure that she would be greatly impressed by Mother's ability in painting, her love of music and poetry. I knew she could not fail to note the number of books and periodicals that cluttered every room, for it was fairly difficult to avoid tripping on some of them.

No young bride about to give her first important dinner party could have been in more of a twitter than I. I tried to impress on Liza and Rachel, who were not many years removed from the cornfield and were miserable when forced to wear shoes, the necessity for a perfect dinner, perfectly served. They were not impressed. I cautioned the young ones on their behavior. I did hope that Father would quote from *Uncle Remus* and not from Mr. Dooley. I even dusted off the Barye lion on the piano, vaguely contemplating a slight dissertation on sculpture, ancient and modern.

I scrubbed myself raw and dressed with meticulous care, even to the point of blacking my shoes, a feat which, though commendable as usual, left my hands in an extremely unfortunate state. As twilight came on I plastered myself against a front window, and as the darkness deepened began to conjure up gloomy fears that she might not come after all.

Then suddenly she was there!

Dinner went off smoothly, in fact too smoothly; it seemed about normal. Somehow I had expected it to be transformed into one of those dinners we read of in books: soft-footed butlers, wine, brilliant conversation, while I, the perfect host, in white front and tails, easily held the table spellbound with my urbane wit and wisdom. But I just couldn't seem to pull it off, couldn't get started. Perhaps I was too absorbed in keeping my shoe-blacked fingers out of sight and eating with less spillage than usual.

The chief trouble seemed to be that there was no opening, for Mother and Miss Barrowes found each other most congenial. Throughout dinner and afterward they chattered without pause about clothes and food, hats, coffee, the servant problem, books, markets, the weather, and all the other stupid things that grownups talk about, while I hovered vaguely in the background, a completely unnoticed little boy with dirty fingers.

Gradually it dawned on me that there was really a great gap between our ages, she was much nearer my mother's generation than mine. Besides, she was entirely too much interested in hats. During the long evening my beautiful romance melted away. There was no heartbreak, only a slight feeling of disillusionment, but by the time she had left, escorted by Harry, no trace of my infatuation remained.

Next morning, struck by the unwonted splendor of my shoes, I had to really think back and wonder how they had gotten that way—and why.

JAMES THURBER

Here Lies Miss Groby

"You remember her. . . . She was forever climbing up
the margins of books and crawling between their
lines. . . ."

Miss Groby taught me English
composition thirty years ago. It wasn't what prose said that interested Miss Groby; it was the way prose said it. The shape of a
sentence crucified on a blackboard (parsed, she called it) brought
a light to her eye. She hunted for Topic Sentences and Transi-
tional Sentences the way little girls hunt for white violets in
springtime. What she loved most of all were Figures of Speech.
You remember her. You must have had her, too. Her influence
will never die out of the land. A small schoolgirl asked me the
other day if I could give her an example of metonymy. (There
are several kinds of metonymies, you may recall, but the one that
will come to mind most easily, I think, is Container for the Thing
Contained.) The vision of Miss Groby came clearly before me
when the little girl mentioned the old, familiar word. I saw her
sitting at her desk, taking the rubber band off the roll-call cards,
running it back upon the fingers of her right hand, and surveying
us all separately with quick little henlike turns of her head.

Here lies Miss Groby, not dead, I think, but put away on a
shelf with the other T squares and rulers whose edges had lost

their certainty. The fierce light that Miss Groby brought to English literature was the light of Identification. Perhaps, at the end, she could no longer retain the dates of the birth and death of one of the Lake poets. That would have sent her to the principal of the school with her resignation. Or perhaps she could not remember, finally, exactly how many Cornishmen there were who had sworn that Trelawny should not die, or precisely how many springs were left to Housman's lad in which to go about the woodlands to see the cherry hung with snow.

Verse was one of Miss Groby's delights because there was so much in both its form and content that could be counted. I believe she would have got an enormous thrill out of Wordsworth's famous lines about Lucy if they had been written this way:

> A violet by a mossy stone
> Half hidden from the eye,
> Fair as a star when ninety-eight
> Are shining in the sky.

It is hard for me to believe that Miss Groby ever saw any famous work of literature from far enough away to know what it meant. She was forever climbing up the margins of books and crawling between their lines, hunting for the little gold of phrase, making marks with a pencil. As Palamides hunted the Questing Beast, she hunted the Figure of Speech. She hunted it through the clangorous halls of Shakespeare and through the green forests of Scott.

Night after night, for homework, Miss Groby set us to searching in "Ivanhoe" and "Julius Caesar" for metaphors, similes, metonymies, apostrophes, personifications, and all the rest. It got so that figures of speech jumped out of the pages at you, obscuring the sense and pattern of the novel or play you were trying to read. "Friends, Romans, countrymen, lend me your ears." Take that, for instance. There is an unusual but perfect example of Container for the Thing Contained. If you read the funeral oration unwarily —that is to say, for its meaning—you might easily miss the C. F. T. T. C. Antony is, of course, not asking for their ears in the sense that he wants them cut off and handed over; he is asking for the function of those ears, for their power to hear, for, in a word, the thing they contain.

At first I began to fear that all the characters in Shakespeare and Scott were crazy. They confused cause with effect, the sign for the thing signified, the thing held for the thing holding it. But after a while I began to suspect that it was I myself who was crazy. I would find myself lying awake at night saying over and over, "The thinger for the thing contained." In a great but probably misguided attempt to keep my mind on its hinges, I would stare at the ceiling and try to think of an example of the Thing Contained for the Container. It struck me as odd that Miss Groby had never thought of that inversion. I finally hit on one, which I still remember. If a woman were to grab up a bottle of Grade A and say to her husband, "Get away from me or I'll hit you with the milk," that would be a Thing Contained for the Container. The next day in class I raised my hand and brought my curious discovery straight out before Miss Groby and my astonished schoolmates. I was eager and serious about it and it never occurred to me that the other children would laugh. They laughed loudly and long. When Miss Groby had quieted them she said to me rather coldly, "That was not really amusing, James." That's the mixed-up kind of thing that happened to me in my teens.

In later years I came across another excellent example of this figure of speech in a joke long since familiar to people who know vaudeville or burlesque (or radio, for that matter). It goes something like this:

> A: What's your head all bandaged up for?
> B: I got hit with some tomatoes.
> A: How could that bruise you up so bad?
> B: Those tomatoes were in a can.

I wonder what Miss Groby would have thought of that one.

I dream of my old English teacher occasionally. It seems that we are always in Sherwood Forest and that from far away I can hear Robin Hood winding his silver horn.

"Drat that man for making such a racket on his cornet!" cries Miss Groby. "He scared away a perfectly darling Container for the Thing Contained, a great, big, beautiful one. It leaped right back into its context when that man blew that cornet. It was the most wonderful Container for the Thing Contained I ever saw here in the Forest of Arden."

"This is Sherwood Forest," I say to her.

"That doesn't make any difference at all that I can see," she says to me.

Then I wake up, tossing and moaning.

MAZO de la ROCHE

All Things Lovely

. . . I had woken with the feeling that I had left
something of myself submerged in the dream, and
also that I had brought something out of it which
would somehow make me different.

Upstairs I showed her my Christ-
mas presents: the doll with bisque face, arms and feet and white
kid body, the toys, the books. She held the doll in her arms for an
ecstatic moment, then— "Can you sew?" she asked.

I had to acknowledge that I could not.

"I can sew," she said, "and I can recite 'The Jackdaw of
Rheims,' all the way through. Should you like to hear me?"

She began at once:

> The jackdaw sat in the Cardinal's chair,
> Bishop and friar and monk were there—

And on to the end in her small clear voice.

A delicious intimacy was there between us, in that chill upstairs, with the grownups far below and the January sunset red-
dening the walls. Never before had I had a child in the house
with me, a child who would go to bed when I went, have in common with me the activities of childhood. I was used to being made
much of, the only grandchild on either side of the family, but I

longed for a companion of my own age. Here was the perfect one.

I brought out my Christmas books, the favourite *Through the Looking-Glass*. We sat together at a table close to the window to catch the last of the daylight and read aloud, page about. I remember how carefully we sounded the *g* in gnat, our heads—hers fair, mine curly and brown—touching, our legs, in their long black cashmere stockings, dangling. . . .

"I'll tell you my secret," I had said to Caroline that January evening when we had sat together reading *Through the Looking-Glass*. "I call it my play, but now you are here, we shall play it together—if you think you can."

"I can play anything—if it's pretend," she had said. "I've never tried it, but I know I can."

So then I had told her.

First it had been a dream, an extraordinarily vivid dream, out of which I had woken with the feeling that I had left something of myself submerged in the dream, and also that I had brought something out of it which would somehow make me different. I cannot now remember what happened in the dream, but I well remember the characters who took part in it and have no reason to forget them, for I have known them ever since. . . .

Caroline seemed not in the least surprised when I told her of these characters. She sat there in the wintry twilight, tiny, fragile, receptive as a crystal goblet held beneath a tap. When I told her the names of the six characters, she said, "Yes, yes, I'll remember." Never did she forget, either those or their personal appearances, which I minutely described.

The room grew darker. Through the clear space I had scratched on the frosty pane, I could see the new moon riding in the white surf of clouds. All is clearly etched in my memory. . . .

When I was nine someone gave me copies of a young people's

71

paper. It was, I think, the *Youth's Companion*. In it was announced a short-story competition for children of sixteen and under.

Unconcerned by my youngness, I set out at once to enter the competition. Optimistic, though easily downcast, I saw no reason why I should not be the winner. With foolscap paper, pen and ink I began to write, and so on and on till eight pages were filled. The story was about a lost child named Nancy. Terrible times she went through but at last was restored to her mother's arms—my own heart ready to burst with emotion as I finished the story with a text from the Prodigal Son.

"But darling," said my mother, "do you think a child would ever be so hungry she would eat potato parings?"

"Nancy was," I said firmly.

"And do you think her mother would quote a text the moment her child was given back to her? It sounds so pompous."

This was my first experience of criticism, and how it hurt!

My father, standing by, exclaimed, "I'm dead sure I'd eat potato peelings if I were hungry enough and as for the text—it was the proper thing for the mother to quote. Don't change a word of it. It will probably get the prize."

Off he went to the letter box to post the manuscript. . . .

Many years afterward I found, among my mother's things, the manuscript of "Nancy" and the letter from the editor— "You are very young to have entered the competition but, if the promise shown by this story is fulfilled, you will make a good writer yet." Dear, oh dear!

Caroline and I were sent to a small private day school kept by a gentle and charming Irish woman. I do not think I learned very much, but I spent happy hours there. Already I could read and this had opened up a new world, the world of books. I owned a great pile of books for children—*Alice in Wonderland* and

Through the Looking-Glass, The Water Babies, The Little Duke, the Kate Greenaway books; these were my favourites. In those days the child had not the excitement of moving pictures and television. The young fancy was not spread out thin over many interests but concentrated on a few, and if he took to books, what a world of delight lay before him! At that time my Uncle Danford's business took him to London every year and each time he brought me a new book, a doll or a dress from a London shop.

By the time I was ten I read every book that came my way—*Oliver Twist* several times, *Old Curiosity Shop* once, for I hated Quilp and, even then, found the death of Little Nell too sentimental. But when our teacher read aloud *Misunderstood,* I was so overwhelmed that the reading had to be stopped. One of my uncles was given a book called, I think, *The Adventures of Hadji Baba.* He was no reader, but, on my next visit to Grandpa's, I found it, and "devour" is the only word which expresses my absorption in the adventures. I have no recollection of the story, but I remember Grandpa's discovery of the book, his brief scanning of it, his striding to the kitchen and before the frightened eyes of the maid, Victoria, taking off a stove lid and thrusting the book onto the coals. In fascination I had followed him. "But, please, sir," quavered Victoria, "why did you burn that nice book?"

"It was not a nice book, Victoria," answered Grandpa. "It was a very nasty book and I will not have my son tempted to read it."

Little did he dream that the small granddaughter, standing innocently by, was thanking her stars that she had finished the book before its destruction. I believed Grandpa when he said the book was wicked, but I could not believe that it had hurt me to read it. I concluded that what might be harmful to a young man could not hurt a small girl.

Other books of those days come crowding into my mind: *Car-*

rots—Just a Little Boy, Spoilt Guy, Little Women—though I liked *Little Men* still better—*The Bastables* by E. Nesbit. . . .

The new furnishings transformed our apartment in the hotel. Handsome carpets took the place of dun-coloured ones, long reseda-green curtains hung at each one of the deep windows, with their built-in seats for which Kay's had made fitted cushions. These stand out in my memory because of the hours I spent curled up in them, the curtains drawn between me and the outer world, reading, reading, reading.

And there was plenty to read. We had brought a few books with us—the volumes of Shakespeare which my father's father had sent him on his twentieth birthday—the heavy calf-bound volumes of Johnson's dictionary which had been sent him when he was seventeen. I am ashamed to say that I once sold the Shakespeare, illustrated by steel engravings and with favourite passages marked by my grandfather. It was one of those impulsive things I have so often done and often regretted.

My father had bought a bookcase and handsome sets of Dickens and Scott. Even while I admired the new furniture I could not keep my eyes from the books. How happy we were going to be in Galt! . . .

About this time I gave up childish reading. I spent my happiest hours in one of the deep window seats living with the novels of Dickens and Scott—*David Copperfield, A Tale of Two Cities, Rob Roy, Quentin Durward*. My mother cared little for Scott, but she delighted in Dickens, the Brontës, Jane Austen. Another favourite of hers was Rhoda Broughton, though what pleased me most in her books was their lovely titles—*Red as a Rose Is She* and *Cometh up as a Flower*.

All three of us read everything that came our way, with uncritical zest. Often my father and I read the same book at the same time, his six feet three extended in an easy chair, my growing length draped against his chest. So I remember reading *The White Company, Harry Lorrequer, Allan Quatermain* by Rider Haggard. In this last book there was a young warrior named, I think, Umslopogaas, whom we very much admired. From this time, for many years, my father called me by this name. In fact, he had a variety of names for me, beginning from the time the news of my conception was first broken to him. The three of us, and, later, Caroline, had secret names for each other that the outside world never knew.

I think it was in these days, when first we began to read together, that the bond between my father and me strengthened into a deep understanding and we became the most loved of friends. As he waited for my slower grasp of the page to catch up to his, as his large shapely hand was raised to turn the page, a palpable emotion stirred within us. My love for my mother was instinctive. I took her devotion for granted. But he was my hero, my protector, my gay companion. . . . As I grew older and young men appeared on the scene, I invariably compared them to him, to their disadvantage—till the day when one arrived who could better bear comparison with him.

Evenings in front of the fire in our living-room we in turn entertained each other. My mother would recite a poem by Tennyson, her violet eyes dimmed by emotion as she enunciated:

> Break, break, break,
> On thy cold gray stones, O Sea!
> And I would that my tongue could utter
> The thoughts that arise in me.

The trouble was that she would recite the verses in the wrong order.

"That's not right, Bertie," my father would interrupt. "You have them in the wrong order."

"Who is reciting this poem?" she would cry.

"You are," he would growl, "but you've got it wrong."

"I can prove I'm right."

Simultaneously they would pounce on the volume of Tennyson. Then he would recite "The Wreck of the *Julie Plante*" and my mother and I would listen entranced, picturing the sinking of the little vessel "wan arpent from de shore." Meanwhile the pug sat on his knee, its prominent eyes fixed mournfully on his face.

I could scarcely bear to wait for my turn. I stood up taut, declaiming:

> 'Twas brillig, and the slithy toves
> Did gyre and gimble in the wabe. . . .

It was not enough for me to recite the "Jabberwocky." I must act it. Once I snatched up an ivory paper knife and, as I cried:

> One, two! One, two! And through and through
> The vorpal blade went snicker-snack!

I flourished the knife and somehow—I never knew how it happened—the blade struck the back of my mother's hand and great red drops of blood came spurting out. In consternation, in shock, I threw down the paper knife and bent over her hand. With eyes full of concern for my pain, she cried:

"It's nothing—it didn't hurt at all!"

One evening my mother said to my father, "We should do some serious reading. It will be good for us and good for Mazo to hear. There are those volumes of Shakespeare your father gave you. Let's read one of the plays aloud."

"We've seen Irving and Ellen Terry in them," he said. "And Robert Mantell. That ought to be enough."

"That will not help our child. It will be splendid for her to hear us read them. Let's begin with *Othello*. I'd love to do Desdemona. You can be the Moor. We'll divide up the other characters."

He became as enthusiastic as she. They drew chairs to the table and laid the volume before them. The pug and I were audience.

At first the reading went well. Then my father read words that made my mother recoil. She cried, "Oh, you shouldn't read that—not in front of her!" and she cast a solicitous look at me.

"How was I to know what was coming?" he demanded.

"Anyone could see what was coming!"

"Why didn't you stop me, then—before I said it?"

"I tried to stop you but I couldn't."

"Anyhow," said my father tranquilly, "she wouldn't understand—not any more than that pug."

My mother cast doubtful looks on both me and the pug, and we, feeling embarrassed, slunk into the next room.

My mother was always trying to protect my innocence, while my father seemed to think it was its own protection. His favourite author was Balzac and he encouraged me to read him. Together we discussed *Père Goriot*. Tears were in my father's eyes. He was easily moved to laughter, but tears were not embarrassing to him. I remember, when we went to see Martin Harvey in *The Only Way*, how we cried together at Sidney Carton's last words—"It is a far, far better thing that I do than I have ever done. It is a far, far better rest that I go to, than I have ever known." To see a play with my father, to be moved to emotion, either happy or sad, in his company, was to me a pleasure not to be oudone by any in the company of my contemporaries. He and I read books together, drove together, walked together. I contrasted him with the fathers of my friends, who were often stern or fault-finding or repressive. The thought of sternness or punishment in connection with him was unthinkable. As for my mother, she always wanted me to do what I wanted to do! Yet both were high-tempered people.

As for me—their offspring—I am weak as water, always only too ready to be guided by those I love, my only defense the ability, like water, of sometimes slipping from under.

MARY ELLEN CHASE

Recipe for a Magic Childhood

. . . my mother's voice brought trooping into our
kitchen all those with whom we rejoiced or suffered,
admired or feared, loved or hated.

As I write these words at the
kitchen table of an old Connecticut farmhouse above a quiet
valley, a January snowstorm is whitening the brown fields beyond
the windows and the gray stone walls surrounding them. A gravel
road leads from the farmhouse to one of the main Connecticut
highways along which cars and trucks are doubtless speeding;
but since I can neither see nor hear them, I can be pleasantly unaware of their existence. The red-and-white-checked cloth of this
kitchen table, the wood fire burning in the iron range, the smell
of a pot roast taking its time in the oven—all these suggest an
earlier time and, perhaps, a less confusing and problematical
existence. At all events, once I had seated myself at this table and
looked out upon the drifting snowflakes, I found the book which
I am supposed to review intolerably dull and determined instead
to write some desultory paragraphs about other January snowstorms, about another kitchen, and about books not dull at all.
For January snowstorms are always indissolubly connected in my
mind with those I knew in Maine many years ago, and any

79

kitchen, by comparison or by contrast, is equally closely connected with the one in which I was literally brought up.

In Maine country villages, at the beginning of the present century, the kitchen of all homes was the center of their activities. It was not only the one room in the house sure to be warm, but also the one place where a mother, inevitably dedicated to its never-ending rites and ceremonies, could keep an eye on her children. Country winters in my childhood also added to a mother's responsibilities, for in Maine, at least, there was no school during January and February. Whether this Long Vacation, as we called it, was made necessary by municipal poverty, or whether rural school boards then had more confidence in the educational value of parents than many school boards, rural and urban, entertain at present, I do not know; but, happily for us, the situation persisted throughout my childhood. In January and February our village schoolhouse remained closed and frigid and we, when snowstorms or bitter weather made coasting and skating impossible, went to school in our mothers' kitchens.

Our Maine kitchen was large and sunny, with red geraniums in its eastern windows and from its western a wide view of fields and hills. Jutting from its south wall was our huge black wood stove, known by its name in raised iron letters across its oven door as The Rising Sun; and my mother kept it shining by a polish called by the selfsame name. Between the eastern windows stood our kitchen table with a red-and-white-checked cloth to match the geraniums, and by one of the windows was a Boston rocker, also painted red and flanked by four small red stools, which were pushed under the table when not in use. The black iron kitchen sink separated the two western windows and held on its right shelf a green pump, which often had to be "caught" by a dipper of water drawn from the water pail on the shelf to the left. Against the north wall, opposite the stove and affording a view from both eastern and western windows, was the piece of furniture which most intimately concerned us children. This was what we termed the "secretary." It was in reality a high and heavy chest of six drawers, with two stout and wide shelves above them. The upper shelf had on either side a stout carved post; the lower, below two smaller drawers, was just the right height from the upper to serve as a perfect footrest for small feet.

My mother was a versatile young woman, as she had need to be with four children before she had reached the age of thirty; and she early saw in the old secretary an indispensable ally. Even in a kitchen as large as ours four pairs of feet about the floor could be not only an intolerable nuisance, but a possible source of perils to her and to us; and, long before I can remember, she had solved this problem by elevating us all to the top shelf of the secretary. A roller towel, carefully placed beneath the armpits of the two children on the right and then around the convenient post; a similar securing of the two on the left; and we were proof against any cold drafts across the yellow painted floor, against kettles of hot fat, and, best of all, against the possible boredom of any number of January snowstorms.

I spent innumerable winter mornings on the top of that old secretary with my two sisters and my brother. I can still smell the warm spicy smells of gingersnaps baking in the oven, of apple pies rich with cinnamon, and of countless doughnuts merrily bobbing about on the surface of boiling fat. My mother sang hymns as she went about her work and often encouraged us to sing with her. One of her favorites was "Shall we Gather at the River?" and all of us, joining in the chorus, loved to assure her that we most certainly would gather there. "Yes, we'll gather at the river, the beautiful, the beautiful river," we would all shout together, each, I feel sure, thinking of that river only as some pleasant family picnicking ground on some pleasant, undefined day in the future. When the old clock in our dining room slowly struck eleven, my mother reached up to each of us a fresh cooky and a cup of milk; and we laid aside our spool knitting machines or the books we were reading for this midmorning excitement.

It is always with books that the old secretary associates itself in my mind, for we read for hours there, sometimes the older of us aloud to the younger while they were still unable to read, sometimes, after we had all learned the magic of words, by ourselves. And we learned this magic very early, not waiting to be taught at school. Without doubt, since we possessed a father who when at home was almost never without a book in his hand, and a mother who somehow found time to read as well as to darn and cook, fashion clothes and refashion them, clean and wash and iron, we absorbed while still very young the wholesome truth that books held manifold riches which we must discover for ourselves. And, since fortunately the four of us were separated by only a few years, we could share this discovery without too much responsibility one for another. There we would sit for hours upon our lofty perch while the snow fell or bitter winds blew across our white fields, not actually upon the secretary at all, but instead in Arabia with Aladdin or in the dark forest with Hansel and Gretel, with the four ingenious Robinsons on their mysterious island or with Oliver Twist in the workhouse, with David Copperfield on the Peggottys' houseboat, loving the alluring smell of crabs and lobsters and the blue mug holding a nosegay of seaweed, or with Jim Hawkins, crouching in the apple barrel of the Hispaniola.

My mother usually somehow managed, at eleven, to sit down for half an hour in the red rocking chair by the window. She called this half hour her "respite," a word which early charmed me; and on days when no drafts were blowing across the floor (for even The Rising Sun was not always victorious over the worst of Maine weather) she would help us down from our Parnassus and allow us to sit upon our red stools while, our cookies and milk consumed, she herself would read aloud to us. Here was the very doorsill to complete enchantment, for she was seemingly as lost as we in whatever she was reading. The iron teakettle simmered on The Rising Sun; the red geraniums glowed with life; smells of our approaching dinner filled our noses from stewpans or baking dishes; while my mother's voice brought trooping into our kitchen all those with whom we rejoiced or suffered, admired or feared, loved or hated.

Nor did she bring them among us only by her voice. Seemingly she became as distressed as we over their misfortunes, as angry as we over their misdeeds. "Isn't he a wicked man?" she would cry when Fagin terrified Oliver in the dark attic; and, suiting her behavior to her disgust and loathing, she would slap the passage which chronicled such horrid goings-on. Then nothing would do but that we should each in turn slap the page, she solemnly allowing us this expression of righteous indignation.

There was always the excitement of our father's coming home at noon, stamping the snow from his overshoes, shaking his coat in the entry, commenting on the storm or cold. He was always interested, as he lifted us down from the secretary, in our morning, in what we had been reading; and if he was not too encumbered by the ways and means of feeding both our bodies and our small heads, he would sometimes promise to go on that evening with an especial book, reading to us himself by the living-room fire while my mother, as avid a listener as we, should darn the countless socks and patch the red flannel underwear.

It is not only in tribute to the old secretary that I write of its blessings, but even more in tribute to two young parents, who knew well that in opening the wide doors of reading to their children, they were building for them houses not made with hands, dwelling places of the mind, which would always furnish them with food, shelter and delight. My mother and father, to be sure, were not faced fifty years ago with the battle of books against the conflicting forces of the radio, the movies, comics and television; and yet had they been, they would not, I think, have been too dismayed. After all, even in those days, which often seem so far removed from life as we know it, parents had to meet other encroachments upon time, to cope with other intrusions. The endless tasks which faced a woman from dawn until dark in a house quite without "modern conveniences" took a vast toll of both time and energy and often resulted in physical weariness almost inconceivable today. Nor were country villages and even their outlying farm districts in any sense places of monastic seclusion. They had their manifold social gatherings, then as now, their church suppers, school exhibitions, village dramatic societies, whist parties, lodge and Grange get-togethers. Even a far greater measure of neighborliness took its toll of hours and of effort. Then as now, in fact, all families were faced with the ever-present problem of the salvaging of time, with the wise saving of hours to be used for the common benefit and the common pleasure. Had my parents been besieged by pleadings for a television set in the living room or seen The Lone Ranger, or Hopalong Cassidy, or Superman in the process of winning the day over the family reading circle, I rather think they would have met these claimants to our attention and devotion with the only possible weapon then as now—the clear and uncompromising example of their own enthusiasms and values.

They were only in their late twenties when we four children were learning, or had learned, to read; and like most young parents today they loved excitement and were eager after all things new and strange, even in their relatively stable world. Recalling how my father invested money which he could not afford in the first bathroom to appear in our small town, and daily hauled in his neighbors to view his new pride and joy, I am sure that he would have bought a television set; and I am equally sure that my mother's Wednesday and Saturday baking of many loaves of bread would have been vastly enlivened by a radio serial. But I am even more certain that hours for the enjoyment of each would have been strictly defined and clearly understood and that neither would even have been allowed to usurp the place of books and reading in our common life.

For there is no substitute for books in the life of a child; and the first understanding of this simple and irrefutable truth must come from his early perception of his parents' faith in it. They alone can give him this knowledge just as they alone are responsible for the practice of their faith. If they themselves look upon radio programs and the television screen, valuable as certain of their offerings may be, as clearly secondary to the chapter from the bedtime book, and if they good-humoredly insist that neither takes the place of hours spent in quiet reading, the battle for the books is won.

There are many ways in which parents can make clear to children their own respect and love for good reading. The gift of a book or the buying of one from the family budget can easily be made an event in the life of a child. He should be taken to the bookshop on the momentous day of the purchase and allowed to look about on its bright offerings. Taught by example as well as by precept, he will learn the careful handling of such treasures. Once at home and his hands carefully washed before the parcel is opened, the binding of the new book, its illustrations, even its print should be shared with him and the time for its reading discussed. And if in the shop he has been entranced by a comic, as every child I have known in the past decade *has* been entranced, the wise guardian of his destiny will not become either openly disapproving or inwardly too deeply distressed. Most children read comics with their tongues in their cheeks, knowing them, I am convinced, for what they are far better than their elders know them. Parents, I feel sure, worry too much about their baneful influence. The constructive anxiety which results in the quiet substitution of beautiful books for cheap and ugly ones is far more to the purpose.

I would even go so far as to suggest that we concern ourselves much too seriously with *what* a child reads. *That* he reads early and eagerly should be our first concern; and if good books are placed within his reach and he knows, not that they are "good for him," but that his parents once read and loved them, or even still do, he will eventually form his own tastes. In my childhood and young girlhood I was never forbidden to read any book in our relatively small bookcases. I assume that my parents saw to it that none which might be unwise for my eyes and mind was there; but I was never once told that any book was "bad" for me or "too old" for me. I read most of those we owned, novels, poems, biographies, in a "first fine careless rapture"; and once I had done and there was nothing new that I could find, I read them again with almost equal excitement.

Two young parents whom I now know allow their son and daughter, aged eight and ten, to read for an hour every night in bed after they are sent there promptly at eight o'clock. I know of no wiser plan to ensure a love of books and a dependence upon them. The very sight of a book upon his bedside table widens the horizons of a child and affords a spur to his imagination. And a shelf of them of his own, however small in number, kept within reach of his hands, is a possession no child should be without.

The characters in books, as well as those of radio programs, should be household words and their authors should become familiar presences at family tables, a habit which only parents can generate and preserve.

In this connection I can never forget an incident which happened to me in the year 1894 when I was seven years old. In my childhood, Robert Louis Stevenson, or R. L. S. as he was always called, was such a household word, for his stories were read and adored by the parents and children alike of countless American families. My grandmother, who spent much of her time with us and who was herself an avid reader, returned one December morning from a walk to the village. When she entered our kitchen, we saw to our astonishment that she was crying. She sat down in the Boston rocker by the window and to our further amazement covered her face with the black sateen apron which she always wore. "I won't believe it!" she said in response to my mother's questions. "I can't bear it! They say that R. L. S. is dead."

This, I suppose, was the first time in my small life that I had ever realized the devotion which an author can stir within the hearts and minds of his readers, the part that he may forevermore play in their imaginations, the satisfactions he may be capable of granting them. The impression, though perhaps dimly understood, was a lasting one; and I have never forgotten that December day so long ago.

Perhaps I have seemed to speak with undue authority in these paragraphs, written at this kitchen table in this Connecticut farmhouse. For I am still here; the snow still falls on fields now white; the pot roast has long since been eaten and the dishes washed; the short winter day is now, as we say in Maine, "on the edge of darkness"; and the paragraphs have perhaps become far too many.

But I feel that I can speak with more than a little measure of authority, for I have spent forty years of my life in the teaching of literature to boys and girls of grade-school age, to high-school students, and, in the past thirty years, to girls in college. I have, in these years, learned a great deal about the minds and imaginations of the young. I know that, if they have been nurtured and nourished by an early love of books, they have far finer and more sensitive minds and imaginations; and I know, too, that girls (and boys, as well) who possess books will live and will contribute that richness to the communities in which they will become the successful parents of children. I am even convinced that many of the girls whom I teach, or try to teach, have received a better preparation for college in their homes—yes, even in their mothers' kitchens—than they have received at school, provided always that their parents have, even without a massive old secretary as an aid, known how to lift them above what Wordsworth calls "the dreary intercourse of daily life" by leading them early into the paths of books. For through their reading in those most formative years from seven to seventeen they have become all unconsciously the dwellers in many lands, the intelligent and eager associates of all manner of people. Through their early familiarity with words they have gained a facility in speech and in writing which no other source can give. They will never be bored, for they can always seek out a world perhaps at the moment more desirable than the one in which they live and companions often more real than those close at hand. The value of the experiences which they themselves will meet in life can be increased by their knowledge of similar experiences in the realm of books; and the sorrows which they must weather can be made more bearable by the lines of poetry forever in their minds. Every year when they come to me as freshmen I know at once whether or not they come from homes where books have been thought indispensable and where parents have already made their study in college rewarding and delightful.

And now since supper is an hour away and the wood in the cookstove is crackling in preparation, I think I shall fetch my ragged copy of *Oliver Twist* and imagine myself again on the top of the old secretary.

"Please, sir," said Oliver, "I want some more." He was asking for gruel and got but a blow from the ladle instead; yet his words will continue to be spoken by children and wise parents together concerning that better food which is forever theirs for the taking.

Story-Sticks

and Cobwebs Gold

Books are bridges,
Shining, free,
Which link us to
Ourselves-to-be.
　　　　　—Virginia Scott Miner

ANNE PARRISH

For Dillwyn Parrish

Late one night, in winter, in snowy December,
  We started this story, telling it to each other.
Fire was warm and roses smelled sweet, I remember,
  And we whispered, so that we wouldn't waken mother.

Out in the hall the grandfather clock was ticking,
  Petals fell, and the ashes ran with red.
And we heard the wind, and sleet on the windows clicking,
  And mother called to us, "Children, come to bed."

"We'll go on with the story tomorrow—we'll do it together."
  Then we had to go back to our lessons; it didn't get done.
And time has drifted past like a wind-blown feather.
  But wasn't it fun, little brother? Wasn't it fun?

ROBERT P. TRISTRAM COFFIN

Lost Paradise

It was those books on the farm that had got Peter
started off thinking and acting books out underneath
the tall trees, and the story-stick had come out of
them. And part of every breath that Peter drew . . .

In one of Peter's favorite history
books there were pictures of great men of the past. Caesar, Alfred,
Lincoln. But Peter had never yet seen a head as handsome as his
father's head, so upright and so broad across the brows. He knew
he would never find one.

The turnips had to be bagged then and tagged for delivery in
town.

By the time the gunlow load was taken care of, it might be
midnight, and Peter would be very tired. Then the best time of
all came. Peter went in with his father and sat over the stove in
the back room of the shop. The firelight came out through the
cracks in the stove's sides and played in queer designs on the
ceiling. There were three old-fashioned jugs with blue flowers
painted on them hung up there among the beams. The firelight
danced on them, and whole stories out of the *Arabian Nights*
flashed through Peter's drowsing head.

Peter had read all the *Arabian Nights*. Not the abbreviated
versions for boys and girls, but the whole unexpurgated thing. He

had purloined his father's set, on the index for the younger members of the family, from the library shelf, and had read straight
through it, volume by volume, all one Summer, while he stood
sentinel at the fence of the kidney-bean patch. A bull of his
father's had a passion for breaking down fences. He was not an
ugly bull. He just seemed to want to show off his strength before
his she-folks. He never would meddle with a fence if even so
small a human as an eleven-year-old boy was on the horizon. But
just let no one be there, and he walked majestically through the
barbed wire fence and carried off fifty yards of it on his black
shoulders. So Peter's father had Peter stand guard. He never
knew why his son had such starry eyes that Summer. Peter had
lived through the whole of Arabian civilization and a thousand
tales that Summer, sitting with his back to a pine and his face
turned in the bull's direction. The pine boughs with the west
wind in them fitted in with the sound of the wings of great jinns.
The Summer clouds were high domes of Bagdad. And not a
kidney bean was lost.

Now in the late firelight of the shop kitchen, that Summer
was relived by Peter. Great shapes of magic came out over the
ceiling. The boy went over at last completely into the shapes of
mystery and fire. He woke up for a moment to find himself in his
father's arms being carried up to the bed overhead to continue his
dreams. . . .

The game Peter was playing now was trying to think of the
hardest work he had to do on the farm. He was doing his best to
wean himself of thinking of it as a place that was all apple pie
and huckleberry jam. This Thursday morning, he ran over the
unpleasant jobs he had sweated at.

He dismissed sawing wood at once, for he was always able to
prop a book up on the jaws of the sawhorse and read between
sticks. His mother caught him at it once. She thought it was

funny there were such long and regular pauses between saws.
She knew something was up. . . . When his mother came out to
see just why each cordwood length took so long, Peter did not
have time to slide *The Water Babies* under the pile of sticks. His
mother took the book away. After that, that stent at the bucksaw
had been hard work, with nothing but wasp nests to look at between times. But it wasn't usually. Peter had read half of *The
Leatherstocking Tales* in the dim light of the shed and in the
aroma of sawdust. When he was really resting, between every
twenty sticks, there was the mowing machine seat to sit on. . . .
No, he couldn't put down sawing wood as the worst the farm
had to offer. . . .

There was digging clams, of course, on the still days when
the midges were thick as fiddlers in Tophet and stung your eyes
till they looked like two burnt holes in a blanket. But that was
really fishing, and fun. And you got money for doing it—fifty
cents a bushel, and that meant two more books for your own
library, *Black Beauty,* perhaps, or *Heroes of the War of 1812.* . . .

Peter had read through all the History books and all the
Readers in the school. He had read about Zeus and Hera,
Aphrodite and Athena, and knew how they all looked in their
pictures. They all had quiet marble eyes. Peter walked home with
Hermes on one side and Thor on the other. He knew how many
men Stonewall Jackson had at Antietam and just what Peter
Stuyvesant said when the English fleet came up the bay to New
Amsterdam. What did he need to go to Canaan to go to school
for? He knew things years ahead of Miss Pettingill's room. He
knew and felt hard about things Miss Pettingill never would feel
or know about. Peter hadn't stopped at the books. He went on
from where they left off on his walk home through the pinewoods and across the bay with the evening star beside him. The

people he read about were just as real to him as his father was and his brothers. They kept on growing with him. They weren't dead or out of time at all.

There was a pinewoods right in back of the barn on the farm, and when Peter sat there, he could hear Zeus speaking just as clear as he could hear Ansel calling the cows home. It was the sound the light breeze made in the thousands of needles on the boughs. He could hear Thor there, and Thialfi and the bleat of the magic goats. He didn't have to try to hear them. He couldn't help hearing them. The sound in the pines was something like the sound of the strings on his father's guitar, when he plucked them and let them tremble for a long time. Only it never faded out, and it made words. Peter could sit down under those pines, or anywhere, by himself, and in five minutes he would be among his great friends. He couldn't hear a large pine forest going in a big wind without plunging into Homer. Achilles and Hector went to bed by him in the dark at night. If his father was there, that was all the better. Peter could hear them talking in between the words his father said. His father was awfully like the two of them, anyway. And King Arthur's moustache looked for all the world like his father's.

Peter could make up whole new stories out of whole cloth when he was all by himself. That was why he liked to walk so much in the woods on the farm. He had to have a stick in his hand. That was the odd part to the business. The stories wouldn't begin to come, if he didn't have the stick. It wasn't the way it was when he was sitting down. And the stick had to be one that balanced right when Peter swung it. The right heft and swing. He had a dozen of those sticks, polished from long handling, beside the gate leading to the pasture. He kept them hidden there so nobody would see them.

Once Edward found one of the sticks, and mimicked Peter's swinging it. Right before Peter. Peter was so angry and ashamed, too, he couldn't think for half an hour.

Going after the cows was when Peter used the story-sticks most. And it was easier to get going when the light was low and the clouds stood up tall above him like towers and fitted into the stories. It wasn't so easy on the way home from school, no matter if there were woods to help. The other children were there. And no mater how well balanced his stick was, Peter couldn't swing it the way he wanted to. Bringing home the cows was the best time.

Peter was very tall in the stories, and all the great old people out of the books, and new ones, too, whom he was going to put into books himself some day, talked with him man to man. He would come home along the winding cowpath, with heifers and cows streaming in a slow line in front. And elbow to elbow with Peter would be Sir Tristram and Merlin, and maybe Ysolt trailing a train of pearls among the cobwebs on the junipers and in the Queen Anne lace. They might come up to the Old Man of the Sea at the sumach bushes by the turnip patch. And if his brothers and sisters only kept away—especially Edward—Undine might be waiting at the Well Pond, with her white feet in the chickweed. Ansel would say they were only Peking ducks. Peter walked as slow as he could, and keep the cows in sight, as the swallows flew higher and higher and the stars began to kindle in the sky. . . .

But ducks and geese and turnips weren't the only things Peter's father had on his farm. He had books, too. He had a whole room full of them. His favorite book was the Shakespeare one, but he could say a lot of *Paradise Lost,* too. He used to go on for hours. Peter got the habit from him. He could say a lot of poetry at a stretch, too. And he had started out reading right through the whole room. He read every minute he could. Lying on his belly on the hearth—or under the sofa if it was the unexpurgated volumes—Peter read till his head was full. He went through the Inferno with Doré's engravings to make his eyes bug and waded through *Don Quixote* by the light of the same artist's mind. Inferno was much nicer than Paradise. Peter liked the picture where the sinful had their bare legs up through the smoking holes best. In *Don Quixote* his favorite was the picture of the knight cutting the giants in two. Peter loved to see works. And there were a lot of works in a giant's belly. You'd never think a man could have so much in his interior. . . .

The Shakespeare book was worn loose at its back by Peter and his father. The boy would lie on his elbows and listen to his father speaking in Gaunt's voice about England, and kings, and death. Kings and death were favorite subjects of his father, when he got heated up and solemn. There was a lot about Peter's father that was like a king. Anybody could tell that to see his curly hair over his wide forehead in the light of a hearth fire. Anybody could tell that to hear his voice and see the way he held his head up stiff. It was the way he looked when he was mowing. Peter had rather hear his father read Shakespeare than strum his guitar and sing *Belle Brandon,* even. And Peter loved that song. Peter's father had said Shakespeare to him long before he knew what half the words were about. Peter knew from the first, though, that they were about something fine. They sounded like a south gale making the pines roar on a January night. They sounded like the thunder of the mile of surf on Pond Island ledges. They came up from something deep.

"For God's sake, let us sit upon the ground
And tell sad stories of the death of kings:
How some have been deposed, some slain in war,

99

Some haunted by the ghosts they have deposed,
Some poisoned by their wives, some sleeping killed:
All murdered: for within the hollow crown
That rounds the mortal temples of a king
Keeps Death his court. . . ."

That was the way Peter dreamed the world was going to be. Strange and deep and sad, and yet like a kind of music. Some day he would know all about it. Now it was enough to hear his father's deep voice going on and on like a prophecy in the night.

It was those books on the farm that had got Peter started off thinking and acting books out underneath the tall trees, and the story-stick had come out of them. And part of every breath that Peter drew . . .

ELEANOR FARJEON

The Little Bookroom

. . . no wonder that its mottled gold-dust still danced
in my brain, its silver cobwebs still clung to the corners
of my mind.

In the home of my childhood
there was a room we called 'The Little Bookroom.' True, every
room in the house could have been called a bookroom. Our
nurseries upstairs were full of books. Downstairs my father's
study was full of them. They lined the dining-room walls, and
overflowed into my mother's sitting-room, and up into the bed-
rooms. It would have been more natural to live without clothes
than without books. As unnatural not to read as not to eat.

Of all the rooms in the house, the Little Bookroom was yielded
up to books as an untended garden is left to its flowers and weeds.
There was no selection or sense of order here. In dining-room,
study, and nursery there was choice and arrangement; but the
Little Bookroom gathered to itself a motley crew of strays and
vagabonds, outcasts from the ordered shelves below, the over-
flow of parcels bought wholesale by my father in the sales-rooms.
Much trash, and more treasure. Riff-raff and gentlefolk and
noblemen. A lottery, a lucky dip for a child who had never been
forbidden to handle anything between covers. That dusty bookroom, whose windows were never opened, through whose panes

the summer sun struck a dingy shaft where gold specks danced and shimmered, opened magic casements for me through which I looked out on other worlds and times than those I lived in: worlds filled with poetry and prose and fact and fantasy. There were old plays and histories, and old romances; superstitions, legends, and what are called the Curiosities of Literature. There was a book called *Florentine Nights* that fascinated me; and another called *The Tales of Hoffmann* that frightened me; and one called *The Amber Witch* that was not in the least like the witches I was used to in the fairy-tales I loved.

Crammed with all sorts of reading, the narrow shelves rose halfway up the walls; their tops piled with untidy layers that almost touched the ceiling. The heaps on the floor had to be climbed over, columns of books flanked the window, toppling at a touch. You tugged at a promising binding, and left a new surge of literature underfoot; and you dropped the book that had attracted you for something that came to the surface in the upheaval. Here, in the Little Bookroom, I learned, like Charles Lamb, to read anything that can be called a book. The dust got up my nose and made my eyes smart, as I crouched on the floor or stood propped against a bookcase, physically uncomfortable, and mentally lost. I was only conscious of my awkward posture and the stifling atmosphere when I had ceased to wander in realms where fancy seemed to me more true than facts, and set sail on voyages of discovery to regions in which fact was often far more curious than fancy. If some of my frequent sore throats were due to the dust in the Little Bookroom, I cannot regret them.

No servant ever came with duster and broom to polish the dim panes through which the sunlight danced, or sweep from the floor the dust of long-ago. The room would not have been the same without its dust: star-dust, gold-dust, fern-dust, the dust that returns to dust under the earth, and comes up from her lap in the shape of a hyacinth. "This quiet dust," says Emily Dickinson, an American poet—

> *This quiet dust was Gentlemen and Ladies,*
> *And Lads and Girls:*
> *Was laughter and ability and sighing,*
> *And frocks and curls.*

And an English poet, Viola Meynell, clearing her ledges of the dust that "came secretly by day" to dull her shining things, pauses to reflect—

> *But O this dust that I shall drive away*
> *Is flowers and kings,*
> *Is Solomon's temple, poets, Nineveh. . . .*

When I crept out of the Little Bookroom with smarting eyes, no wonder that its mottled gold-dust still danced in my brain, its silver cobwebs still clung to the corners of my mind. No wonder that many years later, when I came to write books myself, they were a muddle of fiction and fact and fantasy and truth. I have never quite succeeded in distinguishing one from the other, as the tales in this book that were born of that dust will show. Seven maids with seven brooms, sweeping for half-a-hundred years, have never managed to clear my mind of its dust of vanished temples and flowers and kings, the curls of ladies, the sighing of poets, the laughter of lads and girls: those golden ones who, like chimney-sweepers, must all come to dust in some little bookroom or other—and sometimes, by luck, come again for a moment to light.

WINIFRED WELLES

The Attic

I, the contented living child, ran my exploring hand
along the rows of books, pulling one out here or there,
gathering in my variegated store richly and carelessly,
much as a magpie picks up sparkling bits of stone,
ribbon, or refuse and carries them all home to its nest.

POSSIBLY only a dreamy child can
fully grasp—or wants to—the difference between a family store-
room, an attic, and the public secondhand shop, and perhaps the
difference is important only to herself. But all old junk, even
when it has belonged to strangers, must vibrate in the imagination of sensitive observers with many exquisite overtones. If the
junk consists of objects once loved, used, worn, or made by those
of one's own blood, they assume an inescapable and tender signifi-
cance. Even when the object is ludicrous, one's laughter is gentle.
A child wandering among such outcast but still surviving fragments of other times, other lives, sees herself not as an isolated
figure, shelterless and undirected, but as a partaker, a marcher in
a long processional that has passed under this, her very own roof.
Death is diminished for her, and life enlarged. For better or for
worse, the incidents of her own hearth reach out and merge in the
events of her country's history. She comes to have both a respect
and a disregard for Time that are somewhat Chinese. She knows

that the past and the future are closely integrated, yet as distinctly separate as the two sides of a medal, and that her appreciation of the present is measured by the strength of her desire to hold that medal in the hollow of her hand, to scrutinize it, to remember, and to dream.

And so the attic in my grandfather's house became more than just another room in the house. It was the very breath and body of the whole eventful rooftree. Like a family memory-book, it contained a keepsake for everybody, from someone's old doll to someone else's rusty sword. There was a bride's bouquet crumbling to dust in a box, and near by, where it had been set on a shelf neatly tied up in a package, was the groom's hat, the crushable kind, and I was endlessly amused pushing it open and smashing it shut. . . .

One large square trunk held some of the pretty belongings of a belle of the 1870's—pale pink and blue brocades with bustles and pearl trimmings on the bodices, thin silver bangles, rosebud earrings of coral, a feather fan with pearl sticks, and a small black-lace parasol, the ivory handle delicately carved. To complete this gay chapter in her life, as I afterwards learned it downstairs, there should have been one other item that was missing—a pair of slippers with the heels stripped off.

She had had a devoted but jealous beau, evidently a serious fellow who not only writhed at the sight of her dancing with other men but disapproved altogether of the idea of dancing. So, after what must have been rather a high-pitched scene, he stole a pair of her slippers, tore off the heels, and left them in a reproachful little heap outside her door. I used to wonder where the heels were. Had she thrown them away, chagrined? Or did she indignantly bear them off to the shoemaker's to be put back on and to end their days in the polka? . . .

Another trunk held the children's clothes, the hem-stitched

lawn bonnets, the woolen petticoats with scalloped edges, and the long embroidered christening robes of infancy. Some of these things had their stories too, like that one of the little boy just old enough in the year 1849 to say plaintively, "I want a new pair of boots, a pair that *squeaks!*" And there they were to prove the story. . . .

How many times they must have said, "What shall we do with this?" after the ball, the wedding, the christening, the funeral—and the answer appears to have been always the same— "Ah, well, put it away in the attic." It became almost a family refrain. It seems as if such a weight of Time must have pressed the old house farther and farther down into the earth on which it stood. And the books, and the letters—it is almost impossible to describe the quantity or the curiosity or the pathos of those. . . .

Under the eaves, amid a heap of packing-cases, there was a small haircloth trunk, its rounded top studded with brass nails. It contained packets of letters, neatly arranged according to date, from the nineteen-year-old boy who had died in the Battle of Antietam. With the letters, according to the morbid sentiment of the time, was the bullet that gave him the fatal one of his several wounds. On the cover of the box containing it his mother had written in her delicate Victorian hand "The Minnie Ball that killed my son."

That soldier's letters had a strange and very strong fascination for me. They laid on my heart so keen a personal emotion about the Civil War that it seemed like no other war ever waged on earth. I read them so often and with such unmistakable signs of suffering that it became a family joke. "Where's Sister?" one brother would ask, and the other would reply, "Aw, she's up in the attic bawling over the Civil War."

They never saw that soldier as I did. They had their own heroes in the family past, like Philemon Hale, the privateer who gave his crew a mixture of rum and gun-powder before attacking a British ship, or Jonathan Adgate, a surgeon in the Revolutionary Army. So the Civil War soldier, his letters and his memory, became my own. . . .

The books in the attic had been stacked or piled or shoved in anywhere with no attempt at arrangement. Over on the shelves by the door was an assortment including everyone's primers and grammars, English, Latin, French, and Greek. There were Bibles, of course, ranging in size from one no bigger than your thumb to one so large and bulky that I carried it in my arms when I took it across to the window to read. On the flyleaf of that one, in bold, black handwriting, was a man's name, the year 1629, and the words "Essex, England." The other big books, bound in worn leather, were an Apocrypha with engravings and several volumes of the laws of early Connecticut with very stately lettering. There were sermons and treatises and Sunday-school books. There was a grimly illustrated *Medical History of the Civil War,* in which I could see for myself, if I had doubted it, that "they all had terrible wounds." Two volumes contained startling pictures, and accounts of heroic ladies who went along with their husbands in the Union Army. Their hair hung loosely and untidily on their shoulders, like Indians' locks, whether they were in dashing riding-costume with a seven-shooter at the belt or wore trousers like the men, surmounted by a modest knee-length tunic, and carried a sergeant's straight sword.

Evidently someone in the family, or perhaps more than one, had been interested in all kinds of extraordinary women for a long time. A shabby old book called *A Vindication of the Rights of Women* lay at the bottom of a heap, but it had no pictures, and its long, antique *s*'s made it difficult reading. A fat volume labeled *Eminent Women of the Age* in gold letters was less puzzling. And there were portraits of them all too, everyone from Queen

Victoria to Rosa Bonheur, from Julia Ward Howe and Margaret Fuller Ossoli to Mrs. Sigourney. Mrs. Sigourney had lived in Norwich, and I often came on her poems in anthologies or in scrapbooks full of stained clippings.

There was plenty of poetry, both English and American—stout collected works of Tennyson, Byron, and Longfellow, illustrated editions of Whittier and Poe and others. A thin book called *M'Fingal* enchanted me with its humorous pictures. I also dug out of its contents the incredible tale of the British soldiers walking on Beacon Hill at sunset who ran away from June bugs terrified, thinking that they were bullets.

This story, like that one told me by my father of the redcoats who fled in the night from Windham because the bullfrogs sounded like an approaching army, convinced me that the English must be an easily scared nation. But I felt sure that the frogs of Windham had been a mighty race, for the strength of their song was the subject of several legends. These, and many more about all the towns of Connecticut, I found in one book with both covers and some of the pages gone. Somehow such curious trivia lodged in the corners of my mind, like inescapable, queer-shaped pieces of some big picture puzzle that I was trying to reassemble.

I learned that Norwich was once called "The Rose of New England," and that she was famous for the size of her puddings, while New London was noted for that of her dumplings. I often sat wondering what it would have meant to be a guest at tripe suppers, turtle entertainments, or the ordination parties where the clergy displayed such enthusiasm and skill in making punch. But these meditative moments were the mild ones. I read faster when I came to stories of wolves in the swamps around New London, or of the huge black snakes in the Norwich Town meadows, or of the Indians who were everywhere.

Those two chiefs, shrewd Uncas and that other with his rip-pling, melodic name, Miantonomo, I never forgot. They hated and feared and admired each other for a long time, but it was Uncas who, with the help of the English, finally won out. Proud of his victory, he was no less proud of his enemy, for as he stood over the body of the slain Miantonomo, he drew out his long knife and, slicing off pieces of the still warm flesh, he ate them and said:

"It is good. It is sweet. It will make my heart strong."

It was somewhat disappointing to find that only one witch had been hanged in Connecticut. But she haunted me because she was only a girl, and her name, Alse, suggested nothing evil. And al-together, she, the wolves, the snakes, and the Indian chiefs seemed as mythical to read about as some of the records left as to the behavior of nature itself in the various townships—as, for in-stance, the mountain in Moodus that "made noises," or "the rock that walked" on the shore near New London, or the island in the Connecticut River that quietly vanished away.

As a contrast to all this wild, dark, mysterious poetry, there were later substantial figures like Sarah Knight, a very lively lady who finally settled down at Norwich. Early in the eight-eenth century she journeyed through New England, keeping a journal as she went. Apparently equally afraid of a "hors" or a "cannoo," she nevertheless managed to traverse much earth and water. Among many observant comments on people and towns, she mentioned divorces—"stand aways," she called them—and considered them entirely "too much in vogue" among both the English and the Indians.

Sometimes, in trying moments, she found it restful to set down her thoughts in verse. Her phrase for this was "Composing my Resentments," and she resorted to it late one night in a Connecticut travern when some quarrelsome topers in the room next to hers kept her too long awake. She lit her candle in despair and wrote:

> I ask thy aid, O potent Rum,
> To charm these wrangling Topers dum.
> Thou hast their giddy brains possesst,
> The man confounded with the Beast—
> And I, poor I, can get no rest.
> Intoxicate them with thy fumes,
> O still their Tongues till morning comes!

The charm worked, for she added that "the dispute soon ended with t'other dram."

Naturally the attic had no scholarly feeling for the sequence of events. On those shelves and in those boxes and trunks, the decades and the centuries all gathered dust impartially together. I, the contented living child, ran my exploring hand along the rows of books, pulling one out here or there, gathering in my variegated store richly and carelessly, much as a magpie picks up sparkling bits of stone, ribbon, or refuse and carries them all home to its nest. If I was interested one minute to think of Lady Fenwick and her crumbling grave on the shore at Saybrook, I was equally so the next to imagine the Duc de Lauzun, that elegant French nobleman, sulking in the village of Lebanon and longing for the gaiety of Newport. That a hundred years and more, brimful of other lives and events, stretched between this lady and this gentleman would not have disconcerted me very much, even had I happened to count them.

In the attic history shrank, but the lives, as I came upon them, seemed distinct and important, each in its own niche. And the place was so cluttered that it took my mind no longer to dart across the decades, and even from war to war, than it took my eyes to glance from the Union soldier's sword across to the cedar-lined medicine chest that had belonged to the Revolutionary doctor. Perhaps the fact that some of my own discarded toys had found their resting-place up here may have assured me that all the other objects in some way belonged to me as well. My own old doll house with one door off, standing as it did beside a broken spinning wheel, perhaps gave me the impression that one was really no more unfamiliar than the other. They were simply companions in disuse. I never seemed to question why either had been saved. I accepted them, as indeed I accepted the whole attic, as a necessary and comprehensible part of the more orderly rooms downstairs—and so too a part of me myself.

ALEXANDER WOOLLCOTT

Reunion in Paris

. . . when the oblivious Anne Parrish crossed the
street to that bookstall, somewhere in fathomless space
a star chuckled—chuckled and skipped in its course.

THIS is a story—a true story—of
an adventure which befell Anne Parrish one June day in Paris. I
mean *the* Anne Parrish, the one who wrote *The Perennial
Bachelor,* the maliciously surgical *All Kneeling,* and that uncomfortably penetrating and richly entertaining novel called *Loads of
Love.* Although she comes of Philadelphia and Delaware people
and has used their backgrounds and folkways for her books, she
herself grew up out in Colorado Springs and it was not until one
summer about ten years ago that she first experienced the enchantment of Paris. It was all new to her—the placid sidewalk cafés,
the beckoning bookstalls along the river wall, the breath-taking
panorama of the city from the steps of Sacré-Coeur, the twisting
alleys of the Marais, murmurous with the footfalls of two thousand years.

No day was long enough for her. But to her husband Paris was
an old story and one Sunday, after they had been to Notre-Dame
for Mass, then to the bird-market, all a-twitter in the June sunlight, and finally (with detours to a dozen bookstalls) to the
Deux-Magots for lunch, he swore he had seen all of Paris he could

bear to see that day. Not one more bookstall, even if there was another only just across the way, all stocked, no doubt, with First Folios of Shakespeare, unrecognized by the witless bookseller, who would part with them at two francs each. Even so, he would sit him down at this table on the *quai* and take no further needless steps that day. From where he sat, obdurately sipping his *fine,* he could see her a-prowl on the riverbank, watch her as she hovered over the rows of books. At last he saw her pounce on one, wave it in triumph, haggle with the vendor, and come back with her purchase under her arm.

Just see what she had found for a franc! It was a flat, pallid, dingy English book for children, called *Jack Frost and Other Stories*. He inspected it without enthusiasm, implying by his manner that, personally, he would rather have had the franc. But she explained that, valueless as this admittedly insipid volume might seem to him, she was delighted to have it because it was a book she had been brought up on in her nursery days and she had not seen a copy since. For her it would provide material for just such a debauch of memory as I myself might enjoy if ever I could come upon a certain dilapidated volume of *Chatterbox,* from which I was wrenched by harsh circumstance nearly forty years ago. But he was skeptical. Could she, for instance, recall a single story in the lot? Yes, she could. After a spasm of concentration, she fished up out of her memory the fact that one of the stories concerned a little girl named Dorothy—she could even remember the pen-and-ink illustration—a little girl named Dorothy who did not like her own nose.

This bit of testimony confounded him, for indeed there was such an item in the inane collection. There, you see! While she was basking in this triumph, he turned the dog's-eared pages in quest of further data. There was a moment of silence while her glance drifted along the river to the close-packed green of its islands and the towers beyond. This silence was broken abruptly by his admitting, in a strained voice, that after all he was inclined to think she *had* known the book in her younger days. He handed it to her, open at the fly-leaf. On the fly-leaf was penciled in an ungainly, childish scrawl: "Anne Parrish, 209 N. Weber Street, Colorado Springs."

Well, that is the story. How and when the book had first passed out of her possession, she could not recall, if indeed she ever knew. She did not remember having seen or thought of it in twenty years. She could only surmise by what seemingly capricious circumstances and against what dismaying, incalculable odds it had made its journey across five thousand miles of land and sea to take up its place on the bank of the Seine and wait there for the right day and hour and moment in June when she would come drifting by and reach out her hand for it.

Surely the finding of it gave her more deeply nourishing pleasure than any collectors' item—any mere First Folio, for instance—could possibly have afforded her. Pleasure for her and pleasure, too, I think, for all of us. In fact, what interests me most about this story is a result of my own experience in hearing it and, from time to time, telling it. There is something so curiously tickling, so warming to the foolish heart in the phenomenon we call coincidence that the most indifferent stranger is somehow delighted by Anne Parrish's adventure, delighted and cheered by a strong and probably valid sense of good fortune.

I know that when I myself first heard it, I walked down the street in quite a glow, for all the world as if I had just found a tidy sum on the pavement. I had to keep reminding myself that my affairs were, when examined separately and coldly, in just about as parlous a state as they had been before. If the tidings of so uncommon a coincidence thus have all the tingle of good news, if they come to us with the force of a boon and a benison, it is, I suppose, because they carry with them the reassuring intimation that this is, after all, an ordered universe, that there is, after all, a design to our existence. When we thus catch life in the very act of rhyming, our inordinate pleasure is a measure, perhaps, of how frightened we really are by the mystery of its uncharted seas. At least, I know that when I first heard the tale, I carried it about with me as a talisman, more than half disposed to believe that when the oblivious Anne Parrish crossed the street to that book-stall, somewhere in fathomless space a star chuckled—chuckled and skipped in its course.

One Ever

Memorable Day

Cross—for heroes
Left behind
Golden spurs
For you to find!

—Virginia Scott Miner

JOHN KEATS

On First Looking into Chapman's Homer

Much have I travelled in the realms of gold,
  And many goodly states and kingdoms seen;
  Round many western islands have I been
Which bards in fealty to Apollo hold.
Oft of one wide expanse had I been told,
  That deep-browed Homer ruled as his demesne:
  Yet did I never breathe its pure serene
Till I heard Chapman speak out loud and bold:
Then felt I like some watcher of the skies
  When a new planet swims into his ken;
Or like stout Cortez when with eagle eyes
  He stared at the Pacific—and all his men
Looked at each other with a wild surmise—
  Silent, upon a peak in Darien.

E. E. CUMMINGS

Ever Memorable Day

One ever memorable day . . . sage and ignoramus
were sitting opposite each other . . . the ignoramus
listening, enthralled; the sage intoning, lovingly and
beautifully, his favorite poems.

My own home faced the Cam-
bridge world as a finely and solidly constructed mansion, pre-
ceded by a large oval lawn and ringed with an imposing white-
pine hedge. Just in front of the house itself stood two huge
appletrees; and faithfully, every spring, these giants lifted their
worlds of fragrance toward the room where I breathed and
dreamed. Under one window of this room flourished (in early
summer) a garden of magnificent roses: the gift of my parents'
dear friend "stubby" Child—who (I learned later) baptized me
and who (I still later discovered) was the Child of English and
Scottish Ballads. As a baby, I sported a white sweater; on which
my mother had embroidered a red H, for Harvard.

Our nearest neighbor, dwelling (at a decent distance) behind us,
was Roland Thaxter; primarily the father of my loveliest play-
mate and ultimately the professor of cryptogamic botany. To our
right, on Irving Street, occurred professors James and Royce and
Warren; to our left, on Scott Street, transpired professor of eco-

nomics Taussig. Somewhat back of the Taussig house happened professor Lanman—"known and loved throughout India" as my mother would say, with a pensive smile. She had been slightly astonished by an incident which embellished her official introduction to Mr and Mrs Lanman: the celebrated Sanscrit scholar having, it seems, seized his would-be-interlocutor's hand, yanked her aside, and violently whispered "do you see anything peculiar about my wife?"—then (without giving my mother time to reply) "she has new shoes on" professor Lanman hissed "and they hurt her!" I myself experienced astonishment when first witnessing a spectacle which frequently thereafter repeated itself at professor Royce's gate. He came rolling peacefully forth, attained the sidewalk, and was about to turn right and wander up Irving, when Mrs Royce shot out of the house with a piercing cry "Josie! Josie!" waving something stringlike in her dexter fist. Mr Royce politely paused, allowing his spouse to catch up with him; he then shut both eyes, while she snapped around his collar a narrow necktie possessing a permanent bow; his eyes thereupon opened, he bowed, she smiled, he advanced, she retired, and the scene was over. As for professor Taussig, he had a cocker spaniel named Hamlet; and the Taussig family always put Hamlet out when they played their pianola—no doubt the first law of economics —but Hamlet's hearing was excellent, and he yodelled heartrendingly as long as the Hungarian Rhapsody persisted. Genial professor Warren's beautiful wife (whose own beautiful name was Salomé Machado) sometimes came to call on my maternal grandmother; and Salomé always brought her guitar. I remember sitting spellbound on our upstairs porch among appleblossoms, one heavenly spring afternoon, adoring the quick slim fingers of Salomé Machado's exquisite left hand—and I further remember how, as Salomé sang and played, a scarlet tanager alighted in the blossoms; and listened, and disappeared.

One of the many wonderful things about a home is that it can be as lively as you please without ever becoming public. The big Cambridge house was in this respect, as in all other respects, a true home. Although I could be entirely alone when I wished, a varied social life awaited me whenever aloneness palled. A father and mother—later, a sister—two successive grandmothers and an aunt (all three of whom sang, or played the piano, or did both, extremely well) and one uncle, plus three or four hearty and jovial servants, were at my almost unlimited disposal. The servants—and this strikes me as a more than important point—very naturally enjoyed serving: for they were not ignobly irresponsible impersons, they were not shamelessly overpaid and mercilessly manipulated anonymities, they were not pampered and impotent particles of a greedy and joyless collective obscenity. In brief: they were not slaves. Actually, these good and faithful servants (of whom I speak) were precisely everything which no slave can ever be—they were alive; they were loved and loving human beings. From them, a perfect gnoramus could and did learn what any unworld will never begin to begin to so much as suspect: that slavery, and the only slavery, is service without love.

After myself and my father and mother, I loved most dearly my mother's brother George. He was by profession a lawyer, by inclination a bon vivant, and by nature a joyous human being. When this joyous human being wasn't toiling in his office, or hobnobbing with socalled swells at the Brookline country club, he always became my playfellow. No more innocently good-hearted soul ever kissed the world goodnight; but when it came to literature, bloodthirsty was nothing to him. And (speaking of bloodthirstiness) I here devoutly thank a beneficent Providence for allowing me to live my childhood and my boyhood and even my youth without ever once glimpsing that typical item of an era of at least penultimate confusion—the uncomic nonbook. No paltry supermen, no shadowy spacecadets, no trifling hyperjunglequeens and pantless pantherwomen insulted my virginal imagination. I read or was read, at an early age, the most immemorial myths, the wildest wild animal stories, lots of Scott and quantities of Dickens (including the immortal Pickwick Papers), Robinson Crusoe and The Swiss Family Robinson, Gulliver's Travels, Twenty Thousand Leagues Under The Sea, poetry galore, The Holy Bible, and The Arabian Nights. One city winter I floated through chivalry with Mallory and Froissart: the following country summer—we had by then acquired a farm—I dressed as a Red Indian, slept in a teepee, and almost punctured our best Jersey cow with a random arrow; in emulation of the rightful inhabitants of my wrongful native land.

A gruesome history of the Tower of London had been conscientiously compiled by a prominent British prelate, endowed with what would now be termed sadistic trends; and suddenly this fearful opus burgeoned in our midst. Every night after dinner, if George were on deck, he would rub his hands and wink magnificently in my direction and call to my maiden aunt "Jane, let's have some ruddy gore!" whereupon Jane would protestingly join us in the parlour; and George would stealthily produce the opus; and she would blushfully read; and I would cling to the sofa in exquisite terror. We also read—for sheer relaxation—Lorna Doone (with whom I fell sublimely in love) and Treasure Island (as a result of which, the blind pirate Pew followed me upstairs for weeks; while for months, if not years, onelegged John Silver stood just behind me as my trembling fingers fumbled the electric light chain).

Out of Brookline's already mentioned country club, I readily con-
jured a gorgeous and dangerous play-world: somewhat resem-
bling the three ring circus of the five Ringling brothers; and dedicated by dashing gentlemen to fair ladies and five horses and other
entrancing symbols of luxurious living. George had not been
born into this fashionable cosmos, but he loved it so much that
he learned to smoke cigars: and if he hadn't learned anything, the
cosmos would certainly have welcomed him for his own abundant
self's sake. His own abundant self wrote vers de société; which
he recited at orgies or banquets—I was never sure which—but
also, for my benefit, chez lui. And no sooner had George discovered my liking for verse than he presented me with an in-
estimable treasure entitled The Rhymester—opening which totally
unostentatious masterpiece, I entered my third poetic period.

Poetic period number one had been nothing if not individualistic;
as two almost infantile couplets, combining fearless expression
with keen observation, amply testify. The first of these primeval
authenticities passionately exclaims

O, the pretty birdie, O;
with his little toe, toe, toe!

while the second mercilessly avers

there was a little farder
and he made his mudder harder

—but, alas! a moribund mental cloud soon obscured my vital
psychic sky. The one and only thing which mattered about any
poem (so ran my second poetic period's credo) was what the
poem said; it's socalled meaning. A good poem was a poem which
did good, and a bad poem was a poem which didn't: Julia Ward
Howe's Battle Hymn Of The Republic being a good poem be-

cause it helped free the slaves. Armed with this ethical immutability, I composed canticles of comfort on behalf of the griefstricken relatives of persons recently deceased; I implored healthy Christians to assist poor-whites afflicted with The Curse Of The Worm (short for hookworm); and I exhorted right-minded patriots to abstain from dangerous fireworks on the 4th of July. Thus it will be seen that, by the year 1900, one growing American boy had reached exactly that stage of "intellectual development" beyond which every ungrowing Marxist adult of today is strictly forbidden, on pain of physical disappearance, ever to pass.

The Rhymester diverted my eager energies from what to how: from substance to structure. I learned that there are all kinds of intriguing verse-forms, chiefly French; and that each of these forms can and does exist in and of itself, apart from the use to which you or I may not or may put it. A rondel is a rondel, irrespective of any idea which it may be said to embody; and whatever a ballade may be about, it is always a ballade—never a villanelle or a rondeau. With this welcome revelation, the mental cloud aforesaid ignominiously dissolved; and my psychic sky joyfully reappeared, more vital even than before.

One ever memorable day, our ex-substantialist (deep in structural meditation) met head-on professor Royce; who was rolling peacefully home from a lecture. "Estlin" his courteous and gentle voice hazarded "I understand that you write poetry." I blushed. "Are you perhaps" he inquired, regarding a particular leaf of a particular tree "acquainted with the sonnets of Dante Gabriel Rossetti?" I blushed a different blush and shook an ignorant head. "Have you a moment?" he shyly suggested, less than half looking at me; and just perceptibly appended "I rather imagine you might enjoy them." Shortly thereafter, sage and ignoramus were sitting opposite each other in a diminutive study (marvellously smelling of tobacco and cluttered with student notebooks of a menacing bluish shade)—the ignoramus listening, enthralled; the sage intoning, lovingly and beautifully, his favorite poems. And very possibly (although I don't, as usual, know) that is the reason— or more likely the unreason—I've been writing sonnets ever since.

ELLERY QUEEN

Who Shall Ever Forget?

Oh, unforgettable day! . . . I opened the book with
no knowledge that I stood—rather, I sat—on the brink
of my fate.

THIS is one of the Queens speaking. . . . As a boy my reading habits were pure and innocent. I
confess now that I never read a Nick Carter until I was past
voting age. My literary childhood consisted of Horatio Alger,
Tom Swift, the Viking legends, the multicolored Lang fairy
books, Frank Merriwell, Baseball Joe, the Rover Boys, Tarzan,
The Three Musketeers, Jules Verne, Peck's Bad Boy, and—yes,
the Oz stories. I can reread the Oz books today—and I often do.
Somehow the detection of crime failed to cross my path in all
those happy days, except in the movies—remember "The Exploits
of Elaine" with Arnold Daly as Professor Craig Kennedy,
Creighton Hale as Walter Jameson, Pearl White as Elaine, and
the sinister Sheldon Lewis as The Clutching Hand? The closest
I might have come to fictional blood and thunder in those golden
summers was *Tom Sawyer, Detective*—I say "might have come"
because oddly enough I have no recollection of *Tom Sawyer,
Detective* as part of my boyhood reading.

When I was twelve years old, my family moved from upstate
New York to New York City, and for a time we lived with my

grandfather in Brooklyn. It was in my grandfather's house, in the winter of 1917, that I first met Sherlock Holmes. Oh, unforgettable day!

I was ill in bed when the great moment occurred. In those far-off days I was afflicted periodically with an abscess of the left ear. It came year after year, with almost astronomical regularity—and always, I recall, during the week of school exams. My grandfather had an old turnip of a watch that he used to place flat against my left ear, and it always astounded him to learn that I couldn't hear the tick of his Big Ben even after having had my ear lanced.

I was lying in bed, in a cubbyhole of a room, on just such a day as Dr. Watson has so often described—a "bleak and windy" day with the fingers of winter scratching at the windowpane. One of my aunts walked in and handed me a book she had borrowed from the nearby public library.

It was *The Adventures of Sherlock Holmes.*

I opened the book with no knowledge that I stood—rather, I sat—on the brink of my fate. I had no inkling, no premonition, that in another minute my life's work would be born. My first glance was disheartening. I saw the frontispiece of the Harper edition—a picture of a rather innocuous man in dress coat and striped trousers holding the arm of a young woman in bridal gown. A *love story,* I said to myself—for surely this unattractive couple were in a church and about to be married. The quotation under the illustration—"The gentleman in the pew handed it up to her"—was not encouraging. In fact, there was nothing in that ill-chosen frontispiece by Sidney Paget to make a twelve-year-old boy sit up and take notice—especially with his left ear in agony.

Only an unknown and unknowable sixth sense prompted me to turn to the table of contents—and then the world brightened. The first story—*A Scandal in Bohemia*—seemed to hold little red-blooded promise, but the next story was, and always will be, a milestone.

A strange rushing thrill challenged the pain in my ear. *The Red-Headed League!* What a combination of simple words to skewer themselves into the brain of a hungry boy! I glanced down quickly—*The Man with the Twisted Lip*—*The Adventure of the Speckled Band*—and I was lost! Ecstatically, everlastingly lost!

I started on the first page of *A Scandal in Bohemia* and truly, the game was afoot. The unbearable pain in my ear—vanished! The abyss of melancholy into which only a twelve-year-old boy can sink—forgotten!

I finished *The Adventures* that night. I wasn't sad—I was glad. It wasn't the end—it was the beginning. I had knocked fearlessly on the door to a new world and I had been admitted. There was a long road ahead—even longer than I realized. That night, as I closed the book, I felt that I had read one of the greatest books ever written. And today I marvel how true and tempered was my twelve-year-old critical sense. For in the mature smugness of my present literary judgment, I still consider *The Adventures of Sherlock Holmes* one of the world's masterworks.

I could not have slept much that night. If I slept at all, I merely passed from one dream world to another—with the wide-awake dream infinitely more wondrous. I remember when morning came—how symbolically the sun shone through my window. I leaped from bed, dressed, and with that great wad of yellow-stained cotton still in my ear, stole out of the house and made my shaky way to the public library. Of course it was too early for the library to be open, but I sat on the steps and waited. And though I waited hours, it seemed only minutes until a prim old lady came and unlocked the front door.

But alas, I had no card. Yes, I might fill out this form, and take it home, and have my parents sign it, and then after three days— three days? three eternities!—I could call and pick up my card.

I begged, I pleaded—and there must have been something irresistible in my voice and in my eyes. Thank you now, Miss Librarian-of-Those-Days! These thanks are long overdue. For that gentle-hearted old lady broke all the rules of librarydom and gave me a card—and told me with a twinkle in her eyes where I could find books by a man named Doyle.

I rushed to the stacks. My first reaction was one of horrible and devastating disappointment. Yes, there were books by a Doyle on the shelves—but so few of them! I had expected a whole libraryful —rows and rows of Sherlock, all waiting patiently for my "coming of age."

I found three precious volumes. I bundled them under my arm, had them stamped, and fled home. Back in bed I started to read— *A Study in Scarlet,* the *Memoirs* (with a frontispiece that almost frightened me to death), *The Hound of the Baskervilles.* They were food and drink and medicine—and all the Queen's horses and all the Queen's men couldn't put Ellery together again.

But my doom had been signed, sealed, and delivered in *The Adventures.* The books which followed merely broadened the picture, filled in the indelible details. For who can ever forget that tall, excessively lean man with his razorlike face and hawk's-bill of a nose . . . or his mouse-colored dressing gown and amber-stemmed pipe . . . or the way he paced up and down that legendary room at 221B Baker Street, quickly, eagerly, his head sunk upon his chest . . . or the way he examined the scene of a crime, sometimes on all fours, his nose to the ground. . . .

Who could ever forget that gaunt, dynamic figure and his incisive speech . . . or the mysterious Victorian household appliance called a gasogene . . . or the Persian slipper in which

The Master kept his tobacco and the coal scuttle in which he kept his cigars . . . or the patriotic bullet pocks on the wall and the scraping violin which produced such weird melodies . . . or the hypodermic syringe—what a shock that was to my fledgling sensibilities! . . . or the ghostly hansom cab that loomed out of the London mist—with a twelve-year-old boy clinging by some miracle of literary gymnastics to its back as it rattled off to perilous adventure. . . .

Yes, who shall ever forget?

HAL BORLAND

High, Wide and Lonesome

I had just discovered a world of horizons beyond
horizons. . . . I had found something that would
shape my whole life.

I ACHED for several days. Then I
began to accept it. Next year we would have Christmas. This
year we would have the box from Nebraska. With another
childish fairy tale for me. All right, I told myself, so there
wouldn't be any Christmas this year. And I half wished it would
snow and blizzard so much that Father couldn't get home. Then
we could forget Christmas, till next year. . . .

And something began to straighten out inside of me. Christmas
wasn't presents. It wasn't even talking about Christmas and singing Christmas songs. It was something that happened deep down
in you, some happiness you had or those around you had. And the
inner ache began to fade. . . .

Then it hit me. This was Christmas Eve.

All that wall I had built up began to crumble. It was Christmas
Eve and there wasn't going to be any Christmas. Tomorrow
would just be Monday. I gritted my teeth and bit my lip and
pulled the covers over my head. I scrooched down and put my
feet on the hot flatiron wrapped in a towel and I fought the tears.

I thought of Gary and the people talking and laughing, full of Christmas. I thought of all the Christmas things. I had heard without listening and I had seen without looking, and it was almost too much to fight down. Then I heard the sound of Father's voice and slowly the hurt began to relax away. Tomorrow was only Monday, but Father was home. That was our Christmas this year, Father being home. . . .

Mother said, "What's this?"

"Just something I picked up." Father couldn't hide his grin.

"Will, you didn't!"

"Open it," he said to me.

I started to tear the brown wrapping paper. Mother said, "Will, you promised."

"It's not a Christmas present," Father said. "It's something I meant to get when I got back from the mountains."

I tore the paper enough to reveal a gun barrel. I ripped the rest of it. There was the stock. A shotgun, a .12 gauge shotgun. And a box of shells for it.

I stood there speechless.

"Know how to put it together?" Father asked. He showed me. I stood there holding it, and he said, "It's not for Christmas. It's for—well, for last Summer. And for taking care of things—while I was sick." He turned to Mother. "Ed paid me a little extra for the overtime, and—and he can use it this Winter to, well, to help out at the table. It's—it's just a second-hand gun." . . .

I said, "Thank you. I wanted a shotgun more than anything else in the world, but—"

"You earned it, I guess. I suppose you'll want to go hunting."

"Can I?"

"Wait till after dinner and I don't think your mother will mind." . . .

I was at least three miles from home when I saw a thread of

smoke over the next rise half a mile away. It must be from the Bromley place, I thought. . . .

Then, just as I topped the rise, another big white-tail lunged out of the snow right in front of me. I was lucky. I led him just right and he went end over end. I'd got my first rabbit with the new gun.

I was running down the slope to pick up my rabbit when I heard a man shouting. I looked up and there was the Bromley house just below me, a little white-painted house, and a tall, stooped man was standing in the doorway shouting, "Hello! Hello! Come on in! Merry Christmas!"

I picked up my rabbit, proud as a young Indian who had killed his first fat buffalo cow, and went down to the house.

Mr. Bromley had on a store-bought suit and a white shirt. I left my rabbit in the snow outside the door and went inside. The house was as big as ours, but it looked smaller because the bedroom was partitioned off, not just curtained, and there was a rug on the floor and lace curtains at the windows. It was full of savory cooking smells. Mrs. Bromley, a tall, slender woman with gray in her hair, had on a city dress. Both of them were old folks; they must have been in their forties. She greeted me and took my mackinaw and she urged me to sit down.

I sat on the edge of a chair beside a book case and a few minutes later Mrs. Bromley brought a cup of hot cocoa and a plate of cookies. Then they both sat down and began to ask questions.

I drank cocoa and ate cookies and told them who I was, and that Father was a printer, and that we came from Nebraska. And I told them about my new gun and the rabbit.

"You are rather young, aren't you?" Mrs. Bromley asked, "to be out hunting alone. Aren't you afraid you will get lost?"

I smiled. I never got lost.

Mr. Bromley said, "You are talking to a young plainsman,

Alice, not to a city boy. A direct descendant of Daniel Boone and Kit Carson." He smiled.

I don't know what she answered, but she didn't laugh. I wasn't paying much attention, because I had seen the books in that book case beside me. There must have been thirty or forty books. One group of them were all alike except their titles. They were large red books with figures of Indians and frontiersmen outlined on their covers.

Mrs. Bromley was talking to me, asking, "Do you read?" and I remembered my manners.

"Yes ma'am," I said. "I read everything. I've read hundreds of stories in magazines Jack Clothier gave me. He's a cowboy from over at the Lazy Four, but he's gone to Wyoming now."

"Have you ever read Cooper?" she asked. "James Fenimore Cooper."

"No ma'am." I wasn't sure whether that was the name of a book, a magazine, or an author.

"Or Scott? Or Dickens?"

"No ma'am."

"I think you might like them," she said. She took one of the large red volumes from the shelf and handed it to me. I opened it and began to read "The Last of the Mohicans."

I don't know how long I read. At eleven a boy can immerse himself completely in Cooper newly discovered. Mr. and Mrs. Bromley, their house, the plains themselves, were completely forgotten. But at last I heard Mrs. Bromley saying, "Here's another cup of cocoa to warm you on your way. You must start home before dark or your mother will worry. And you might get lost."

I put down the book and drank the cocoa, still in the woods with Hawkeye and Uncas. Then I put on my mackinaw, and Mrs. Bromley gave me a little package of cookies for my pocket.

And she asked, "Would you like to take a book with you?"

I didn't have to answer. She saw my face. She took the book I had been reading, wrapped it carefully and said, "Put it inside your coat and keep it dry. When you've finished it, bring it back and get another."

I picked up my shotgun, remembered to say my thanks, and started for home over the hills where the purple shadows of early dusk already lay deep across the snow.

I was halfway home before I emerged from the story of Uncas and a land I had never seen or heard of, before I really saw the Colorado plains and felt the numbing cold of that Christmas evening. Then I remembered that I had left my rabbit beside the Bromley doorway. The first rabbit I had shot with my new gun.

The quick of a boy's being is close to the surface. I began to cry, excusing the tears because my hands were cold and I was bitterly disappointed. I wanted so desperately to be a man and a provider. Father had given me the gun so we could have meat for the table.

The thoughts of boyhood are at once so simple and so complex, and the feelings can be so deep, so immediate. He hasn't yet calloused himself with adulthood. The world is at once close about him and remote as the stars; it is friendly, and intimate, and hopelessly baffling. He hasn't yet made his compromises with it.

I had just discovered a world of horizons beyond horizons, a world I couldn't see even from the top of the hay stack on a clear day. I had found something that would shape my whole life. It was too late now to go back for the rabbit, and as I trudged on I began to sense my discovery, a discovery even bigger than the plains. The tears stopped and I hurried on home, hugging both the gun and the book.

GRAHAM GREENE

The Lost Childhood

But in childhood all books are books of divination,
telling us about the future, and like the fortune teller
who sees a long journey in the cards by death or water
they influence the future.

PERHAPS it is only in childhood
that books have any deep influence on our lives. In later life we
admire, we are entertained, we may modify some views we already hold, but we are more likely to find in books merely a confirmation of what is in our minds already: as in a love affair it is
our own features that we see reflected flatteringly back.

But in childhood all books are books of divination, telling us
about the future, and like the fortune teller who sees a long
journey in the cards or death by water they influence the future.
I suppose that is why books excited us so much. What do we ever
get nowadays from reading to equal the excitement and the
revelation in those first fourteen years? Of course I should be interested to hear that a new novel by Mr. E. M. Forster was going
to appear this spring, but I could never compare that mild ex-
pectation of civilized pleasure with the missed heartbeat, the ap-
palled glee I felt when I found on a library shelf a novel by Rider
Haggard, Percy Westerman, Captain Brereton or Stanley Weyman which I had not read before. No, it is in those early years

that I would look for the crisis, the moment when life took on a new slant in its journey towards death.

I remember distinctly the suddenness with which a key turned in a lock and I found I could read—not just the sentences in a reading book with the syllables coupled like railway carriages, but a real book. It was paper-covered with the picture of a boy, bound and gagged, dangling at the end of a rope inside a well with the water rising above his waist—an adventure of Dixon Brett, detective. All a long summer holiday I kept my secret, as I believed: I did not want anybody to know that I could read. I suppose I half consciously realized even then that this was the dangerous moment. I was safe so long as I could not read—the wheels had not begun to turn, but now the future stood around on bookshelves everywhere waiting for the child to choose—the life of a chartered accountant perhaps, a colonial civil servant, a planter in China, a steady job in a bank, happiness and misery, eventually one particular form of death, for surely we choose our death much as we choose our job. It grows out of our acts and our evasions, out of our fears and out of our moments of courage. I suppose my mother must have discovered my secret, for on the journey home I was presented for the train with another real book, a copy of Ballantyne's *Coral Island* with only a single picture to look at, a coloured frontispiece. But I would admit nothing. All the long journey I stared at the one picture and never opened the book.

But there on the shelves at home (so many shelves for we were a large family) the books waited—one book in particular, but before I reach that one down let me take a few others at random from the shelf. Each was a crystal in which the child dreamed that he saw life moving. Here in a cover stamped dramatically in several colours was Captain Gilson's *The Pirate Aeroplane*. I must have read that book six times at least—the story of a lost civilization in the Sahara and of a villainous Yankee pirate with an aeroplane like a box kite and bombs the size of tennis balls who held the golden city to ransom. It was saved by the hero, a young subaltern who crept up to the pirate camp to put the aeroplane out of action. He was captured and watched his enemies dig his grave. He was to be shot at dawn, and to pass the time and keep his mind from uncomfortable thoughts the amiable Yankee pirate played cards with him—the mild nursery game of Kuhn Kan. The memory of that nocturnal game on the edge of life haunted me for years, until I set it to rest at last in one of my own novels with a game of poker played in remotely similar circumstances.

And here is *Sophy of Kravonia* by Anthony Hope—the story of a kitchen-maid who became a queen. One of the first films I ever saw, about 1911, was made from that book, and I can hear still the rumble of the Queen's guns crossing the high Kravonian pass beaten hollowly out on a single piano. Then there was Stanley Weyman's *The Story of Francis Cludde,* and above all other books at that time of my life *King Solomon's Mines.*

This book did not perhaps provide the crisis, but it certainly influenced the future. If it had not been for that romantic tale of Allan Quatermain, Sir Henry Curtis, Captain Good, and, above all, the ancient witch Gagool, would I at nineteen have studied the appointments list of the Colonial Office and very nearly picked on the Nigerian Navy for a career? And later, when surely I ought to have known better, the odd African fixation remained. In 1935 I found myself sick with fever on a camp bed in a Liberian native's hut with a candle going out in an empty whisky bottle and a rat moving in the shadows. Wasn't it the incurable fascination of Gagool with her bare yellow skull, the wrinkled scalp that moved and contracted like the hood of a cobra, that led me to work all through 1942 in a little stuffy office

in Freetown, Sierra Leone? There is not much in common between the land of the Kukuanas, behind the desert and the
mountain range of Sheba's Breast, and a tin-roofed house on a
bit of swamp where the vultures moved like domestic turkeys
and the pi-dogs kept me awake on moonlight nights with their
wailing, and the white women yellowed by atebrin drove by to
the club; but the two belonged at any rate to the same continent,
and, however distantly, to the same region of the imagination—
the region of uncertainty, of not knowing the way about. Once I
came a little near to Gagool and her witch-hunters, one night in
Zigita on the Liberian side of the French Guinea border, when
my servants sat in their shuttered hut with their hands over their
eyes and someone beat a drum and a whole town stayed behind
closed doors while the big bush devil—whom it would mean
blindness to see—moved between the huts.

But *King Solomon's Mines* could not finally satisfy. It was not
the right answer. The key did not quite fit. Gagool I could recognize—didn't she wait for me in dreams every night in the passage by the linen cupboard, near the nursery door? and she con-
tinues to wait, when the mind is sick or tired, though now she is
dressed in the theological garments of Despair and speaks in
Spenser's accents:

> The longer life, I wote the greater sin,
> The greater sin, the greater punishment.

Yes, Gagool has remained a permanent part of the imagination,
but Quatermain and Curtis—weren't they, even when I was only
ten years old, a little too good to be true? They were men of
such unyielding integrity (they would only admit to a fault in
order to show how it might be overcome) that the wavering per-
sonality of a child could not rest for long against those monu-
mental shoulders. A child, after all, knows most of the game—it

is only an attitude to it that he lacks. He is quite well aware of cowardice, shame, deception, disappointment. Sir Henry Curtis perched upon a rock bleeding from a dozen wounds but fighting on with the remnant of the Greys against the hordes of Twala was too heroic. These men were like Platonic ideas: they were not life as one had already begun to know it.

But when—perhaps I was fourteen by that time—I took Miss Marjorie Bowen's *The Viper of Milan* from the library shelf, the future for better or worse really struck. From that moment I began to write. All the other possible futures slid away: the potential civil servant, the don, the clerk had to look for other incarnations. Imitation after imitation of Miss Bowen's magnificent novel went into exercise books—stories of sixteenth-century Italy or twelfth-century England marked with enormous brutality and a despairing romanticism. It was as if I had been supplied once and for all with a subject.

Why? On the surface *The Viper of Milan* is only the story of a war between Gian Galeazzo Visconti, Duke of Milan, and Mastino della Scala, Duke of Verona, told with zest and cunning and an amazing pictorial sense. Why did it creep in and colour and explain the terrible living world of the stone stairs and the never quiet dormitory? It was no good in that real world to dream that one would ever be a Sir Henry Curtis, but della Scala who at last turned from an honesty that never paid and betrayed his friends and died dishonoured and a failure even at treachery—it was easier for a child to escape behind his mask. As for Visconti, with his beauty, his patience and his genius for evil, I had watched him pass by many a time in his black Sunday suit smelling of mothballs. His name was Carter. He exercised terror from a distance like a snowcloud over the young fields. Goodness has only once found a perfect incarnation in a human body and never will again, but evil can always find a home there. Human nature is not black and white but black and grey. I read all that in *The Viper of Milan* and I looked round and I saw that it was so.

There was another theme I found there. At the end of *The Viper of Milan*—you will remember if you have once read it— comes the great scene of complete success—della Scala is dead, Ferrara, Verona, Novara, Mantua have all fallen, the messengers pour in with news of fresh victories, the whole world outside is cracking up, and Visconti sits and jokes in the wine light. I was not on the classical side or I would have discovered, I suppose, in Greek literature instead of in Miss Bowen's novel the sense of doom that lies over success—the feeling that the pendulum is about to swing. That too made sense: one looked around and saw the doomed everywhere—the champion runner who one day would sag over the tape; the head of the school who would atone, poor devil, during forty dreary undistinguished years; the scholar . . . and when success began to touch oneself too, how- ever mildly, one could only pray that failure would not be held off for too long.

One had lived for fourteen years in a wild jungle country with- out a map, but now the paths had been traced and naturally one had to follow them. But I think it was Miss Bowen's apparent zest that made me want to write. One could not read her with- out believing that to write was to live and to enjoy, and before one had discovered one's mistake it was too late—the first book one does enjoy. Anyway she had given me my pattern—religion might later explain it to me in other terms, but the pattern was already there—perfect evil walking the world where perfect good can never walk again, and only the pendulum ensures that after all in the end justice is done. Man is never satisfied, and often I have wished that my hand had not moved further than *King Solomon's Mines,* and that the future I had taken down from the nursery shelf had been a district office in Sierra Leone and twelve tours of malarial duty and a finishing dose of blackwater fever when the danger of retirement approached. What is the good of wishing? The books are always there, the moment of crisis waits, and now our children in their turn are taking down the future and opening the pages. In his poem "Germinal" A. E. wrote:

> *In ancient shadows and twilights*
> *Where childhood had strayed,*
> *The world's great sorrows were born*
> *And its heroes were made.*
> *In the lost boyhood of Judas*
> *Christ was betrayed.*

SHERWOOD ANDERSON

New Worlds

We went in and there the room was. . . . Why, how
could there be so many books in the world? . . . My
imagination had built the little study of a small-town
schoolmaster into a kind of palace.

THEN another hard winter: now
our father has a new occupation. He is going from door to door
in the town and to nearby farmers, trying to sell books. One of
the books is *The Memoirs of General Grant*. Another is a book
about the Civil War, about a soldier called Si Klegg. This was
an occupation my father must have liked. It took him into many
houses. He could sit and talk to people for hours.

But no, dear reader, I am not going to spin for you still another
story about my father. How unscrupulously I have used all my
family, particularly my father! Once I had a letter from a reader.
"It may be true that your father would not work," it ran, "but
you have sure worked him." In fact, I have used him so imagina-
tively, letting my fancy play over his figure, that none of my
brothers seem able to recognize him in my writings. No, dear
reader, my aim in this book is to tell another sort of story, a story
of a mind groping, in the end perhaps reaching expression in an
art, of what then happens to the work of art itself, how it in its
turn must grope, trying to find its own life.

As I was saying, our father was selling books. And I was reading them. There was a passage in General Grant's *Memoirs* to be long remembered.

General Grant had been a failure in life but then war came and he was put in command of soldiers in a time of war.

With his regiment he was sent to a certain valley where there was an encampment of the enemy. He was marching at the head of his regiment, along a road up the side of a hill that would lead into a valley beyond. He was suddenly afraid. He trembled with fear. Would he be able to do the right thing when it came to the moment of battle?

Now he is doubting himself, is filled with fear. He rides at the head of his regiment over the brow of the hill and behold, the enemy has fled.

The experience taught General Grant something that, he says in his book, he always remembered, that when he was afraid of the other man, it was also likely that the other man was afraid of him. The thought made a deep impression on my boy's mind. What General Grant had said seemed to jerk open a door. All my life the simple thought so simply and directly put down was to be a help.

I read other books, any books I could get my hands on. I went fishing with a book under my arm, went to ball games and read in a book between innings. There being few books in our house, I went book borrowing through the town. The hunger in me found a quick response. Not that we had many intellectuals among us, but there were some, and a few book readers, book lovers. There was the town photographer who loaned me Bellamy's *Looking Backward* which sent me off into youthful dreams of a new and beautiful social system in which I might some day live. Other men and women, sensing my passion for books, called me into their houses, "Here, boy. You may read this. Take good care of it. Be sure to bring it back." It was Dickens or Thackeray, and even, now and then, a book of Balzac's.

There were pictures hung on the walls of some of the houses into which I went with boy friends. They were pictures of Emerson, Whittier, Longfellow, Hawthorne. The intellectual life of the northeastern Ohio town was dominated by New England —and there was none of Melville, the greatest of all our pre-Civil-War prose-men. An odd sort of problem got into my mind. I found a certain dryness, hardness, coldness in the pictured faces. My boy's mind connected them oddly with the town preachers, and we of our family were not churchgoers. Nevertheless these pictured book-writers were like the preachers—and in me there was this book passion—

I received a key from the superintendent of our town schools, an often violently angry, big-shouldered Irishman with a great black beard. We boys called him Faker Ginn; it was rumored that he went about peeping through keyholes to catch boys throwing spitballs when their teacher's back was turned. An unfair accusation, I am sure. The old style whipping sort of schoolmaster, he had many times tanned my backside. He hated having you make a fuss about it. You were a boy and did certain things. Punishment was necessary. "For God's sake try to take it like a man." Of course, he didn't say quite that.

There was the Irish schoolmaster then who had taken me into his office. This at the end of the school day. I could hear the other kids trooping down a flight of stairs, going into the great outdoors. "Better to get the strapping and have done with it," I would have been thinking. At least if he strapped me, he would not keep me after school.

"You know it's coming to you?"

"Yes sir."

"Then try to take it like a man."

146

"Yes sir."

He gave it to you vigorously, but if you could take it, it soon stopped.

But the key. There was an occasion when, after such a strapping, at the end of a school day, our schoolmaster took me by the hand.

"Well, that's done. Now you come with me." We went, myself fearfully, through streets to his house, and I remember that it was a brick house on one of our better residence streets. Silently we went along and when we had come to the house, we did not enter by the front door, or by the kitchen door where I had been many times to deliver the family wash, but to a hidden side door that led directly into the schoolmaster's study.

We went in and there the room was. I had never before been in such a room. There were books everywhere. Why, how could there be so many books in all the world? There were shelves of books on all four sides of the room going from the floor to the ceiling. The schoolmaster took a key from a bunch of keys and handed it to me. "It is the key to the outer door to this room." It was the place where he worked, but he was gone all day and often in the evening. I got dimly a sense of something I had never before thought of. In our family, there being seven children, we always living in four- or five-room houses, the rooms in the houses always small, there was not, could not be, such a thing as privacy. . . .

That, compared with the schoolmaster's house— But, dear reader, I am not seeking to ring the changes on the hardships of youth in a house of poverty. . . . I am thinking now entirely of the impression made on a boy's mind by a room, the sense coming to the boy in the room of the schoolmaster.

What? He has a room of his own? He may go into it, sit in here, be undisturbed? The others respect his desire for occasional privacy? A kind of catch in the boy's throat. Will such a thing ever happen to me? Will I also have a place, a room like this?

"Not surely with so many books. I could never read them all. I could never get at what the writers were trying to say."

There was the schoolmaster standing and looking down at me. I dare say I was barefooted, bare-legged, my feet dirty and dusty. It seems to me now, looking back to that moment, that there was a very beautiful rug on the floor. My imagination had built the little study of the small-town schoolmaster into a kind of palace. Now, in my fancy, the room becomes huge. Once, many years later, I was in the library of the Emperor Napoleon, in his palace at Fontainebleau. Now, in my fancy, the schoolmaster's study seems rather like that.

"There is this key. It is to be yours. I have a duplicate. Except to clean and dust, no one except myself ever comes into this room, and I get little enough time here. There is the door leading to a little side porch. If you come and I am not here it will not upset me.

"The idea is that you may come and go in this room as you please." I must, even at that moment, have known that I would never dare do it. "You do not behave yourself very well in school, but I do not know that it matters." Could the man have said such a wise thing to me? "It is possible that you may have a mind. There are few enough real minds in the world. I cannot help you much. It may be there are books here that will be of help.

"You are to come and go as you please. You are to take what books you want to read." I am sure the man said nothing about being careful to return the books, nothing of the danger of getting them dirty.

He went about the town, boasting of me.

"He has read more good books than any grown man of this town. He is educating himself thus. He is getting a better education than we could possibly give him in school."

The Logic
of Elfland

Cross, and conquer
Every foe
All your lifetime
Needs to know.

—Virginia Scott Miner

CAROLYN ELLIS

"Rapunzel! Rapunzel!"

The last words fell on the clovered grass.
We closed the book. . . .*And it came to pass*

In a magic spell, in a secret tower
We sat and wove for a prince's hour

Our long gold hair, while the rose's musk
Scented the pallid summer dusk.

Bees droned, and the wind was still;
The day died, and a whippoorwill

Called. . . .but we sat on and wove,
And the moon curved over us in love.

The stars came out, diamond-bright. . . .
They found us then by lantern light.

ROBERT LOUIS STEVENSON

A Gossip on Romance

It was for this . . . we read so closely, and loved our books so dearly, in the bright, troubled period of boyhood.

IN ANYTHING fit to be called by the name of reading, the process itself should be absorbing and voluptuous; we should gloat over a book, be rapt clean out of ourselves, and rise from the perusal, our mind filled with the busiest, kaleidoscopic dance of images, incapable of sleep or of continuous thought. The words, if the book be eloquent, should run thenceforward in our ears like the noise of breakers, and the story, if it be a story, repeat itself in a thousand coloured pictures to the eye. It was for this last pleasure that we read so closely, and loved our books so dearly, in the bright, troubled period of boyhood. Eloquence and thought, character and conversation, were but obstacles to brush aside as we dug blithely after a certain sort of incident, like a pig for truffles. For my part, I liked a story to begin with an old wayside inn where, "towards the close of the year 17—," several gentlemen in three-cocked hats were playing bowls. A friend of mine preferred the Malabar coast in a storm, with a ship beating to windward, and a scowling fellow of Herculean proportions striding along the beach; he, to be sure, was a pirate. This was further afield than my home-keeping fancy loved to travel, and designed altogether for a larger canvas than the tales that I affected. Give me a highwayman and I was full to the brim; a Jacobite would do, but the highwayman was my favourite dish. I can still hear that merry clatter of the hoofs along the moonlit lane; night and the coming of day are still related in my mind with the doings of John Rann or Jerry Abershaw; and the words "postchaise," the "great North Road," "ostler," and "nag" still sound in my ears like poetry. One and all, at least, and each with his particular fancy, we read storybooks in childhood, not for eloquence or character or thought, but for some quality of the brute incident. That quality was not mere bloodshed or wonder. Although each of these was welcome in its place, the charm for the sake of which we read depended on something different from either. My elders used to read novels aloud; and I can still remember four different passages which I heard, before I was ten, with the same keen and lasting pleasure. One I discovered long afterward to be the admirable opening of *What will he do with It:* it was no wonder I was pleased with that. The other three still remain unidentified. One is a little vague; it was about a dark, tall house at night, and people groping on the stairs by the light that escaped from the open door of a sick-room. In another, a lover left a ball, and went walking in a cool, dewy park, whence he could watch the lighted windows and the figures of the dancers as they moved. This was the most sentimental impression I think I had yet received, for a child is somewhat deaf to the sentimental. In the last, a poet, who had been tragically wrangling with his wife, walked forth on the sea-beach on a tempestuous night and witnessed the horrors of a wreck. Different as they are, all these early favourites have a common note—they have all a touch of the romantic. . . .

ELIZABETH ENRIGHT

Magic Then and Now

So it was that the tale-tellers in the nurseries were
prophets making fearful prophecies. . . .

THE lights along the Hudson
winked like candles; the stars winked in the windy sky. Beyond
our kitchen window to the south, the Claremont Inn sparkled as
merrily as a palace on the night of the Prince's ball. Now and
then I glanced at it as I listened. Frances Moynihan, our cook,
was reading me a story.

"When they got near, they saw that the little house was made
of bread and it was roofed with cake; the windows were transparent sugar."

Frances stopped to catch up on her breathing. Never having
had much schooling, reading was a fearful toil for her. She read
doggedly on one uninflected line, the words all sounding about
the same size and weight, with never a breath between them till
the end of the sentence. None of that mattered to me. The
dragons and princesses emerged unimpaired in my imagination;
the witches and ogres were sufficient to disturb my sleep.

In these pauses there were other sounds beside her heavy
breathing. The alarm clock had a strong loud tick, the ropes of
the dumb waiter switched and slapped within their deep en-
closure, like Rapunzel's braids against the tower wall.

I sat perched on the kitchen stepladder, for Frances had no lap. She was a square elderly woman with short thighs and a large abdomen, no lap. Sometimes on a crowded bus she had had to hold me, and it was an uneasy experience; a constant vigilant effort not to slip.

The laboring voice went on and paused, went on and paused. Went on.

"Gretel gave a push which sent the wicked witch right in, and then she banged the oven door and bolted it. The witch howled horribly but Gretel ran away and left her to perish in misery."

As Frances read I watched her face, not knowing that I saw it, yet now, half a lifetime later, I see it photographically clear: tallow-colored, dewlapped, with eyes as black and active as two crickets. It was a face in which impatience and good nature warred together, above all it was a matter-of-fact practical face. I wonder if she even heard the words she read.

"The Father had not had a single happy day since he had deserted his children in the wood, and in the meantime his wife was dead. So all their troubles came to an end and they lived happily together ever afterward. . . .

"All right. Go on with you now. Get on to bed."

Automatically I begged for one more story, a hollow ritual; I never got another and so went off to sleep accompanied by the cozy parable I had just enjoyed, one of many in which rewards were always given to the good—jewels, suitable marriages, halves of kingdoms—and the evil were punished in straightforward ways: pushed into ovens, ground to powder between millstones, made to dance in red-hot shoes at weddings.

I often think of that rich bedtime fare when I am reading to my youngest son. Opening whatever book he chooses, I find myself declaring something like this: "Jimmy had a red express wagon. His little sister Janie had one, too."

Most of the stories start like that, and almost all hew carefully to sunny reassuring fact. It is never said that the principal characters lived happily ever after, nothing so rash is claimed. It is enough that in the end Buddy's Mommy hugs him when he comes home from school, that Billy's Mommy puts a Band-aid on his wound; that Pammy's Daddy takes her to the zoo. Now and then these sensible sagas are varied with sensible fantasies about semi-human tractors or tugboats, each with a cute, cute name, and there are dozens about semi-human animals, usually rabbits, also having cute names and always wearing clothes.

From the latter it is often a relief to turn to the archetype of all clothed rabbits: the first and only genuine Peter Rabbit, the happy creation of a minor genius named Beatrix Potter, who told his story nearly fifty years ago. He was, though greedy, disobedient, and too curious, a rabbit of integrity: a fictional character who rang true throughout, and was never dull or cute. It is not his fault, nor that of his creator, that with his advent there was unloosed upon the earth a pest of Peter Rabbits. His very name was seized without scruple by many other authors and applied to other and inferior rabbits. A few authors, making a feint at originality, thought of names such as Billy or Bobby or Buster Bunny. All the creatures wore coats and trousers and ranged in character from the saccharine to the sadistic; from the lisping unworldly cottontail to the wham-powie-socko rabbit of the comics, who is out for the quick leaf of cabbage. Who on earth could have guessed, for instance, that among the original Peter's hundreds of literary descendants there would be such a one as that caustic, disenchanted dead-end-kid, Bugs Bunny!

Peter Rabbit was not the only product of Beatrix Potter's talent; there was a hedgehog laundress, a chick who was emotionally a goose, a squirrel who told too many riddles for his own good, and a number of mice, among them Mrs. Tittlemouse, a respectable housewife who worried terribly about disorder, and who would certainly have fainted dead away at the sight of her remote relatives, Mickey and Minnie, jitter-bugging on a lighted screen as big as a barn door.

Despite their curious descendants and impostors the Potter animals live as soundly as they did when Frances Moynihan first read of them to me. (No doubt they added healthy variety to my diet of fabulous perils and granted wishes.) I loved them all, as my children did after me, and as their children in turn will do, I'm sure, for these books, with a few other classics, stand solid as little rocks amid the erratically changing currents of literature for the very young.

But what has happened to the fairy tales? I am not concerned here with the comics, they are a mushroom growth, but with the original, long-lived fairy tales that have been handed down for generations. We do not often read or tell them now. Psychologists insist that it was time these stories fell from favor: that they were too frightening and stimulating for the child, and surely they are right in thinking that.

But I believe there is another reason. I believe that we no longer care for fairy tales because too many of them have come true, and as everybody knows, once magic is persuaded from its legend into life it brings danger with it. Converted to reality it is a two-edged blade. Who should know that better than the people of this century?

It is true that now the palace lights up at a touch, that music and visions come in boxes, that we can leave the earth at will, and talk across the oceans without shouting.

But think of the dragons; they are thick as fleas. They clatter over the farmlands, howl through the tunnels, billow in the streets, growl in the sky. They stalk across battlefields blowing fire, and the Firebird and the Phoenix rise up screaming, jet-propelled.

Think of the ogres; the orges we have feared and suffered in our lifetime, and have slain only to find, as in the stories, that where one orge falls another springs up.

Think of the oven where once the wicked witch was put to pay for all her sins, but in our century these iron doors have closed upon the innocent. It cannot be true! But it is true. So is the genie now appearing in the cloud of smoke; a cloud as high as the sky and shaped like an umbrella to shadow half the world. From within its parting plumes his face looks down on us, still enigmatic. We do not know whether we have released a slave or a destroyer; but already we know that he is mightier than we are.

All these products of magic, from the wonderbox of visions to the gaol that housed the genie, had to be imagined before they could be invented, and before they could be imagined as objects they had to be imagined as symbols. So it was that the tale-tellers in the nurseries were prophets making fearful prophecies: making them in tranquil voices to drowsy listeners, as the rocking chair creaked back and forth, and the last of the fire snapped faintly.

That was in another day, when the earth seemed firmer underfoot, and magic safely unattainable. Ours is a different world and we walk gingerly, we tiptoe lightly on its burning crust and whisper not of dragons.

"Listen," we say at bedtime, and open the book to read, "Jimmy had a red express wagon. His little sister Janie had one, too."

LEWIS MUMFORD

Fact and Fantasy

We did not get rid of the dragon; we only banished
St. George. . . .

THE children of Geddes's gen-
eration and social group were brought up on the Here and Now.
That was the title of one of the first books that came into their
parents' hands; and the able woman who wrote it and edited it,
Mrs. Lucy Sprague Mitchell, was originally a collaborator of
Caroline Pratt . . . a wise spinster, with a vinegary tongue, who
had first established a Play School near Washington Square, on
the theory that play is the best source of education for a child.
Plato himself had held this long before Caroline found it out
for herself; but this admirable pedagogical invention was coupled
in Caroline's mind with the philosophy of Dr. John Dewey and
with the notion that the immediate visible environment, visible
and meaningful, that is, to grownups, is the "real" one in which
the child should live.

Fantasy seemed for Caroline another name for illusion and un-
reality; unconsciously repeating Mr. Gradgrind as well as Plato,
she felt that a child needed above all "facts," building its art and
play around its daily actions and its practical needs, even as
arithmetic was to be based upon playing store and post office.
There is much salutary truth in this doctrine, provided one

doesn't fancy that it covers the entire ground. But I always had secret doubts about the banishment of fantasy and the attempt to narrow reality down to visible objects and observable actions. . . . Nevertheless we were carried away by our generation and thought that the factual and the pragmatic should be specially stressed in dealing with a child. I find our faith a little quaint now.

Geddes's secret world, from the very beginning, was, I am sure, a different one. At five he dreamed of a carrot so big that it would take a steam shovel to dig parts of it out, and a derrick to hoist it. Every day one would get out both the steam shovel and the derrick and go to work on it; for one could feed a whole village with just a small portion of it, and all New York could feed off it daily without using up this immense vegetable. That image gave him pleasure. In the same vein, he felt the world would be delightful if wood were precious and glass and china were hard: if wood broke when you dropped it and you could cut glass with a knife or chop it up: if you couldn't walk on floors any more because they would break—and so on. Ten years later he would write a composition about finding a pair of lynxes with hearts so cold they would turn the lake in summer into a skating pond. (Perhaps they were his parents?)

On Geddes's sixth birthday, as his mother remembers it, he had been over-excited by the party and at the end had hurt himself; so he went to bed weeping bitterly. After his mother had read to him a while, he quieted down and relaxed; and they both watched the clouds in the sky from the window back of his bed. They were large, full-bellied clouds, the kind that seem to have body enough to sustain a world of their own; and the little boy and his mother talked about that beckoning world, picturing the kind of life that was lived there: it became his own very Utopia. Geddes was carried away by the image: the land beyond had become so real to him that neither he nor Sophy was at first aware that the shape of the clouds was changing and the golden colors were fading. . . .

Surely, the minds of children are full of memories and forebodings that anticipate and reinforce these more tangible threats of inhumanity: the wildest folk tale, the most brutal fairy story, do fuller justice to their reality than a factual account of a walk to school; and we fooled ourselves when we thought that any antiseptic efforts of ours to keep the germs of fantasy from incubating could banish the child's sense of the mysterious, the inscrutable, the terrible, the overwhelming. In repressing this life of fantasy and subordinating it to our own practical interests, we perhaps made it take more devious forms, or at least gave the demonic a free hand without conjuring up any angelic powers to fight on the other side. We did not get rid of the dragon; we only banished St. George. . . .

G. K. CHESTERTON

The Logic of Elfland

The things I believed most then, the things I believe
most now, are the things called fairy tales.

My FIRST and last philosophy,
that which I believe in with unbroken certainty, I learnt in the
nursery. I generally learnt it from a nurse; that is, from the
solemn and star-appointed priestess at once of democracy and
tradition. The things I believed most then, the things I believe
most now, are the things called fairy tales. They seem to me to
be the entirely reasonable things. They are not fantasies: compared with them other things are fantastic. . . . Fairyland is
nothing but the sunny country of common sense. It is not earth
that judges heaven, but heaven that judges earth; so for me at
least it was not earth that criticised elfland, but elfland that
criticised the earth. I knew the magic beanstalk before I had tasted
beans; I was sure of the Man in the Moon before I was certain
of the moon. This was at one with all popular tradition. Modern
minor poets are naturalists, and talk about the bush or the
brook; but the singers of the old epics and fables were super-
naturalists, and talked about the gods of brook and bush. That
is what the moderns mean when they say that the ancients did
not "appreciate Nature," because they said that Nature was
divine. Old nurses do not tell children about grass, but about

the fairies that dance on the grass; and the old Greeks could not see the trees for the dryads.

But I deal here with what ethic and philosophy come from being fed on fairy tales. If I were describing them in detail I could note many noble and healthy principles that arise from them. There is the chivalrous lesson of "Jack the Giant Killer"; that giants must be killed because they are gigantic. It is a manly mutiny against pride as such. For the rebel is older than all kingdoms. . . . There is the lesson of "Cinderella," which is the same as that of the Magnificat—*exaltavit humiles*. There is the great lesson of "Beauty and the Beast"; that a thing must be loved *before* it is lovable. There is the terrible allegory of the "Sleeping Beauty," which tells how the human creature was blessed with all birthday gifts, yet cursed with death; and how death also may perhaps be softened to a sleep. But I am not concerned with any of the separate statutes of elfland, but with the whole spirit of its law, which I learnt before I could speak, and shall retain when I cannot write. I am concerned with a certain way of looking at life, which was created in me by the fairy tales, but has since been meekly ratified by the mere facts. . . .

One Day
You Met Them

A man called Mark Twain put them in a book.
. . . One day you met them, and Tom let you
whitewash his fence, and Huck let you touch his
dead cat. And suddenly you knew you were home.

—Louis Redmond

LOUIS REDMOND

Their Boyhood Was Made in America

You learned a lot from Tom and Huck . . . they
taught you one thing you'll never forget. . . .

A MAN called Mark Twain put
them in a book, but they wouldn't stay there. You can't keep boys
like Tom Sawyer and Huck Finn cooped up in a book.

They came busting out of the pages, barefooted and dirty, and
they lit out for the free and open spaces, and they've been romp-
ing around there ever since.

One day you met them, and Tom let you whitewash his fence,
and Huck let you touch his dead cat. And suddenly you knew
you were home.

You threw away your shoes. You cut yourself a fishing pole.
You lay on your belly in the soft moss at the river bank. You
played hookey, you smoked cornsilk, you got sick and you
learned better.

You were trying out freedom, getting the taste and heft of it,
learning to handle it. You were an American growing up.

You learned a lot from Tom and Huck. They showed you how
to make lost marbles come back, and how to cure warts with
rainwater from a hollow stump. You learned what a hoot owl is
saying, and what the wind wants to tell you when it hollers in
the trees at night.

Some of these you forgot later, but they taught you one thing you'll never forget, and it's this:

There is a special quality to being young in America. There is a special air of freedom, a special kind of hopefulness, a deep-down faith that life will turn out good. Every man who remembers how it felt will do all he can to keep that faith alive for those who are young today.

H. L. MENCKEN

Larval Stage of a Bookworm

. . . I wandered into Paradise by a kind of accident.

THE first long story I ever read was "The Moose Hunters," a tale of the adventures of four half-grown boys in the woods of Maine, published in *Chatterbox* for 1887. *Chatterbox*, which now seems to be pretty well forgotten, was an English annual that had a large sale, in those days, in the American colonies, and "The Moose Hunters" seems to have been printed as a sort of sop or compliment to that trade, just as an English novelist of today lards his narrative with such cheery native bait as "waal, pardner," "you betcha" and "geminy-crickets." The rest of the 1887 issue was made up of intensely English stuff; indeed, it was so English that, reading it and looking at the woodcuts, I sucked in an immense mass of useless information about English history and the English scene, so that to this day I know more about Henry VIII and the Lincoln Cathedral than I know about Millard Fillmore or the Mormon Temple at Salt Lake City.

"The Moose Hunters," which ran to the length of a full-length juvenile, was not printed in one gob, but spread through *Chatterbox* in installments. This was an excellent device, for literary fans in the youngest brackets do their reading slowly and painfully, and like to come up frequently for air. But writing down

to them is something else again, and that error the anonymous
author of "The Moose Hunters" avoided diligently. Instead, he
wrote in the best journalese of the era, and treated his sixteen-
year-old heroes precisely as if they were grown men. So I liked
his story very much, and stuck to it until, in a series of perhaps
twenty sessions, I had got it down.

This was in the Summer of 1888 and during hot weather, for
I remember sitting with the volume on the high marble front
steps of our house in Hollins street, in the quiet of approaching
dusk, and hearing my mother's warnings that reading by failing
light would ruin my eyes. The neighborhood apprentices to
gang life went howling up and down the sidewalk, trying to lure
me into their games of follow-your-leader and run-sheep-run, but
I was not to be lured, for I had discovered a new realm of being
and a new and powerful enchantment. What was follow-your-
leader to fighting savage Canucks on the Little Magalloway
river, and what was chasing imaginary sheep to shooting real
meese? I was near the end of the story, with the Canucks all
beaten off and two carcasses of gigantic meese hanging to trees,
before the author made it clear to me that the word *moose* had
no plural, but remained unchanged *ad infinitum*.

Such discoveries give a boy a considerable thrill, and augment
his sense of dignity. It is no light matter, at eight, to penetrate
suddenly to the difference between *to, two* and *too*, or to that
between *run* in baseball and *run* in topographical science, or *cats*
and *Katz*. The effect is massive and profound, and at least comparable to that which flows, in later life, out of filling a royal flush
or debauching the wife of a major-general of cavalry. I must have
made some effort to read *Chatterbox* at the time my Grandmother
Mencken gave it to me, which was at Christmas, 1887, but for a
while it was no go. I could spell out the shorter pieces at the
bottom of columns, but the longer stories were only jumbles of

strange and baffling words. But then, as if by miracle, I found suddenly that I could read them, so I tackled "The Moose Hunters" at once, and stuck to it to the end. There were still, of course, many hard words, but they were no longer insurmountable obstacles. If I staggered and stumbled somewhat, I nevertheless hung on, and by the Fourth of July, 1888, I had blooded my first book.

An interval of rough hunting followed in Hollins street and the adjacent alleys, with imaginary Indians, robbers and sheep and very real tomcats as the quarry. Also, I was introduced to chewing tobacco by the garbageman, who passed me his plug as I lay on the roof of the ash-shed at the end of the backyard, watching him at his public-spirited work. If he expected me to roll off the roof, clutching at my midriff, he was fooled, for I managed to hold on until he was out of sight, and I was only faintly dizzy even then. Again, I applied myself diligently to practising leap-frog with my brother Charlie, and to mastering the rules of top-spinning, catty and one-two-three. I recall well how it impressed me to learn that, by boys' law, every new top had to have a licence burned into it with a red-hot nail, and that no strange boy on the prowl for loot, however black-hearted, would venture to grab a top so marked. That discovery gave me a sense of the majesty of the law which still sustains me, and I always take off my hat when I meet a judge—if, of course, it is in any place where a judge is not afraid to have his office known.

But pretty soon I was again feeling the powerful suction of beautiful letters—so strange, so thrilling, and so curiously suggestive of the later suction of amour—, and before Christmas I was sweating through the translation of Grimms' Fairy Tales that had been bestowed upon me, "for industry and good deportment," at the closing exercises of F. Knapp's Institute on June 28. This volume had been put into lame, almost pathological English by a lady translator, and my struggles with it awoke in me the first faint gutterings of the critical faculty. Just what was wrong with it I couldn't, of course, make out, for my gifts had not yet flowered, but I was acutely and unhappily conscious that it was much harder going than "The Moose Hunters," and after a month or so of unpleasantly wrestling with it I put it on the shelf. There it remained for more than fifty years. Indeed, it was not until the appearance of "Snow White" as a movie that I took it down and tried it again, and gagged at it again.

That second experiment convinced me that the fault, back in 1888, must have been that of either the brothers Grimm or their lady translator, but I should add that there was also some apparent resistant within my own psyche. I was born, in truth, without any natural taste for fairy tales, or, indeed, for any other writing of a fanciful and unearthly character. The fact explains, I suppose, my lifelong distrust of poetry, and may help to account for my inability to memorize even a few stanzas of it at school. It probably failed to stick in my mind simply because my mind rejected it as nonsense—sometimes, to be sure, very jingly and juicy nonsense, but still only nonsense. No doubt the same infirmity was responsible for the feebleness of my appetite for the hortatory and incredible juvenile fiction fashionable in my nonage—the endless works of Oliver Optic, Horatio Alger, Harry Castlemon and so on. I tried this fiction more than once, for some of the boys I knew admired it vastly, but I always ran aground in it. So far as I can recall, I never read a single volume of it to the end, and most of it finished me in a few pages.

What I disliked about it I couldn't have told you then, and I can account for my aversion even now only on the theory that I appear to have come into the world with a highly literal mind, geared well enough to take in overt (and usually unpleasant) facts, but very ill adapted to engulfing the pearls of the imagination. All such pearls tend to get entangled in my mental *vibrissae,* and the effort to engulf them is as disagreeable to me as listening to a sermon or reading an editorial in a second-rate (or even first-rate) newspaper. I was a grown man, and far gone in sin, before I ever brought myself to tackle "Alice in Wonderland," and even then I made some big skips, and wondered sadly how and why such feeble jocosity had got so high a reputation. I am willing to grant that it must be a masterpiece, as my betters allege—but not to *my* taste, not for *me.* To the present moment I can't tell you what is in any of the other juvenile best-sellers of my youth, of moral and sociological hallucination all compact, just as I can't tell you what is in the Bhagavad-Gita (which Will Levington Comfort urged me to read in 1912 or thereabout), or in the works of Martin Tupper, or in the report of Vassar Female College for 1865. I tried dime-novels once, encouraged by a boy who aspired to be a train-robber, but they only made me laugh. At a later time, discovering the pseudo-scientific marvels of Jules Verne, I read his whole canon, and I recall also sweating through a serial in a boys' weekly called *Golden Days,* but this last dealt likewise with *savants* and their prodigies, and was no more a juvenile, as juveniles were then understood, than "Ten Thousand Leagues Under the Sea."

But before you set me down a prig, let me tell you the rest of it. That rest of it is my discovery of "Huckleberry Finn," probably the most stupendous event of my whole life. The time was the early part of 1889, and I wandered into Paradise by a kind of accident. Itching to exercise my newly acquired art of reading, and with "The Moose Hunters" exhausted and Grimms' Fairy Tales playing me false, I began exploring the house for print. The Baltimore *Sunpaper* and *Evening News,* which came in daily, stumped me sadly, for they were full of political diatribes in the fashion of the time, and I knew no more about politics than a chimpanzee. My mother's long file of *Godey's Lady's Book* and her new but growing file of the *Ladies' Home Journal* were worse, for they dealt gloomily with cooking, etiquette, the policing of children, and the design and construction of millinery, all of them sciences that still baffle me. Nor was there any pabulum for me in the hired girl's dog's-eared files of *Bow Bells* and the *Fireside Companion,* the first with its ghastly woodcuts of English milkmaids in bustles skedaddling from concupiscent baronets in frock-coats and cork-screw mustaches. So I gradually oscillated, almost in despair, toward the old-fashioned secretary in the sitting-room, the upper works of which were full of dismal volumes in the black cloth and gilt stamping of the era. I had often eyed them from afar, wondering how long it would be before I would be ripe enough to explore them. Now I climbed up on a chair, and began to take them down.

They had been assembled by my father, whose taste for literature in its purer states was of a generally low order of visibility. Had he lived into the days of my practice as a literary critic, I daresay he would have been affected almost as unpleasantly as if I had turned out a clergyman, or a circus clown, or a labor leader. He read every evening after dinner, but it was chiefly newspapers that he read, for the era was one of red-hot politics, and he was convinced that the country was going to Hell. Now and then he took up a book, but I found out long afterward that it was usually some pamphlet on the insoluble issues of the hour, say "Looking Backward," or "If Christ Came to Chicago," or "Life Among the Mormons." These works disquieted him, and he naturally withheld them from his innocent first-born. Moreover, he was still unaware that I could read—that is, fluently, glibly, as a pleasure rather than a chore, in the manner of grown-ups.

Nevertheless, he had managed somehow to bring together a far from contemptible collection of books, ranging from a set of

Chambers' Encyclopedia in five volumes, bound in leather like the Revised Statutes, down to "Atlantis: the Antediluvian World," by Ignatius Donnelly, and "Around the World in the Yacht *Sunbeam*." It included a two-volume folio of Shakespeare in embossed morocco, with fifty-odd steel plates, that had been taken to the field in the Civil War by "William H. Abercrombie, 1st Lieut. Company H, 6th Regiment, Md. Vol. Inftr.," and showed a corresponding dilapidation. Who this gallant officer was I don't know, or whether he survived the carnage, or how his cherished text of the Bard ever fell into my father's hands. Also, there were Dickens in three thick volumes, George Eliot in three more, and William Carleton's Irish novels in a third three. Again, there were "Our Living World," by the Rev. J. G. Woods; "A History of the War For the Union," by E. A. Duyckinck; "Our Country," by Benson J. Lossing, LL.D., and "A Pictorial History of the World's Great Nations From the Earliest Dates to the Present Time," by Charlotte M. Yonge—all of them likewise in threes, folio with lavish illustrations on steel, stone and wood, and smelling heavily of the book-agent. Finally, there were forty or fifty miscellaneous books, among them, as I recall, "Peculiarities of American Cities," by Captain Willard Glazier; "Our Native Land," by George T. Ferris; "A Compendium of Forms," by one Glaskell; "Adventures Among Cannibals" (with horrible pictures of missionaries being roasted, boiled and fried), "Uncle Remus," "Ben Hur," "Peck's Bad Boy," "The Adventures of Baron Münchhausen," "One Thousand Proofs That the Earth Is Not a Globe" (by a forgotten Baltimore advanced thinker named Carpenter), and a deadly-looking "History of Freemasonry in Maryland," by Brother Edward T. Schultz, 32°, in five coal-black volumes.

I leave the best to the last. All of the above, on my first exploration, repelled and alarmed me; indeed, I have never read some of them to this day. But among them, thumbing round, I found a series of eight or ten volumes cheek by jowl, and it appeared on investigation that the whole lot had been written by a man named Mark Twain. I had heard my father mention this gentleman once or twice in talking to my mother, but I had no idea who he was or what he had done: he might have been, for all I knew, a bartender, a baseball-player, or one of the boozy politicoes my father was always meeting in Washington. But here was evidence that he was a man who wrote books, and I noted at once that the pictures in those books were not of the usual funereal character, but light, loose and lively. So I proceeded with my inquiry, and in a little while I had taken down one of them, a green quarto, sneaked it to my bedroom, and stretched out on my bed to look into it. It was, as smarties will have guessed by now, "Huckleberry Finn."

If I undertook to tell you the effect it had upon me my talk would sound frantic, and even delirious. Its impact was genuinely terrific. I had not gone further than the first incomparable chapter before I realized, child though I was, that I had entered a domain of new and gorgeous wonders, and thereafter I pressed on steadily to the last word. My gait, of course, was still slow, but it became steadily faster as I proceeded. As the blurbs on the slip-covers of murder mysteries say, I simply couldn't put the book down. After dinner that evening, braving a possible uproar, I took it into the family sitting-room, and resumed it while my father searched the *Evening News* hopefully for reports of the arrest, clubbing and hanging of labor leaders. Anon, he noticed what I was at, and demanded to know the name of the book I was reading. When I held up the green volume his comment was "Well, I'll be durned!"

I sensed instantly that there was no reproof in this, but a kind of shy rejoicing. Then he told me that he had once been a great reader of Mark Twain himself—in his younger days. He had got hold of all the volumes as they came out—"The Innocents" in 1869, when he was still a boy himself; "Roughing It" in 1872, "The Gilded Age" in 1873, "Tom Sawyer" in 1876, "A Tramp Abroad" in 1880, the year of my birth, and so on down to date. (All these far from pristine firsts are still in the Biblioteca Menckeniana in Hollins street, minus a few that were lent to neighbor boys and never returned, and had to be replaced.) My father read them in the halcyon days before children, labor troubles and Grover Cleveland had begun to frazzle him, and he still got them down from the shelf on quiet evenings, after the first-named were packed off to bed. But a man of advancing years and cares had to consider also the sorrows of the world, and so he read in Mark less than aforetime.

As for me, I proceeded to take the whole canon at a gulp—and presently gagged distressfully. "Huckleberry Finn," of course, was as transparent to a boy of eight as to a man of eighty, and almost as pungent and exhilarating, but there were passages in "A Tramp Abroad" that baffled me, and many more in "The Innocents," and a whole swarm in "A Gilded Age." I well recall wrestling with the woodcut by W. F. Brown on page 113 of the "Tramp." It shows five little German girls swinging on a heavy chain stretched between two stone posts on a street in Heilbronn, and the legend under it is "Generations of Bare Feet." That legend is silly, for all the girls have shoes on, but what puzzled me about it was something quite different. It was a confusion between the word *generation* and the word *federation,* which latter was often in my father's speech in those days, for the American Federation of Labor had got under way only a few years before, and was just beginning in earnest to harass and alarm employers. Why I didn't consult the dictionary (or my mother, or my father himself) I simply can't tell you. At eight or nine, I suppose, intelligence is no more than a small spot of light on the floor of a large and murky room. So instead of seeking help I passed on, wondering idiotically what possible relation there could be between a gang of little girls in pigtails and the Haymarket anarchists, and it was six or seven years later before the "Tramp" became clear to me, and began to delight me.

It then had the curious effect of generating in me both a great interest in Germany and a vast contempt for the German language. I was already aware, of course, that the Mencken family was of German origin, for my Grandfather Mencken, in his care for me as *Stammhalter,* did not neglect to describe eloquently its past glories at the German universities, and to expound its connections to the most remote degrees. But my father, who was only half German, had no apparent interest in either the German land or its people, and when he spoke of the latter at all, which was not often, it was usually in sniffish terms. He never visited Germany, and never signified any desire to do so, though I recall my mother suggesting, more than once, that a trip there would be swell. It was "A Tramp Abroad" that made me German-conscious, and I still believe that it is the best guide-book to Germany ever written. Today, of course, it is archaic, but it was still reliable down to 1910, when I made my own first trip. The uproarious essay on "The Awful German Language," which appears at the end of it as an appendix, worked the other way. That is to say, it confirmed my growing feeling, born of my struggles with the conjugations and declensions taught at F. Knapp's Institute, that German was an irrational and even insane tongue, and not worth the sufferings of a freeborn American. These diverse impressions have continued with me ever since. I am still convinced that the German language is of a generally preposterous and malignant character.

"Huck," of course, was my favorite, and I read it over and

over. In fact, I read it regularly not less than annually down to my forties, and only a few months ago I hauled it out and read it once more—and found it as magnificent as ever. Only one other book, down to the beginning of my teens, ever beset me with a force even remotely comparable to its smash, and that was a volume called "Boys' Useful Pastimes," by "Prof. Robert Griffith, A.M., principal of Newton High School." This was given to me by my Grandmother Mencken at Christmas, 1889, and it remained my constant companion for at least six years. The sub-title describes its contents: "Pleasant and profitable amusement for spare hours, comprising chapters on the use and care of tools, and detailed instructions by means of which boys can make with their own hands a large number of toys, household ornaments, scientific appliances, and many pretty, amusing and necessary articles for the play-ground, the house and out-of-doors." Manual training was still a novelty in those days, and I suspect that the professor was no master of it, for many of his plans and specifications were completely unintelligible to me, and also to all the neighborhood boys who dropped in to help and advise. I doubt, indeed, that any human being on earth, short of an astrophysicist, could have made anything of his directions for building boat models. But in other cases he was relatively explicit and understandable, and my brother Charlie and I, after long efforts, managed to make a steam-engine (or, more accurately, a steam-mill) according to his recipe. The boiler was a baking-powder tin, and the steam, issuing out of a small hole in the top, operated a sort of fan or mill-wheel. How we provided heat to make steam I forget, but I remember clearly that my mother considered the process dangerous, and ordered us to take the engine out of the cellar and keep it in the backyard.

I had no more mechanical skill than a cow, but I also managed to make various other things that the professor described, including a what-not for the parlor (my mother professed to admire it, but never put it into service), a rabbit-trap (set in the backyard, it never caught anything, not even a cat), and a fancy table ornamented with twigs from the pear tree arranged in more or less geometrical designs. "Boys' Useful Pastimes" was printed by A. L. Burt on stout paper, and remains extant to this day—a rather remarkable fact, for other boys often borrowed it, and sometimes they kept it on their work-benches for a long while, and thumbed it diligently. One of these boys was Johnnie Sponsler, whose father kept a store in the Frederick road, very near Hollins street. Johnnie was vastly interested in electricity, as indeed were most other boys of the time, for such things as electric lights, motors, telephones and doorbells were just coming in. He thus made hard use of Professor Griffith's Part VII, which was headed "Scientific Apparatus and Experiments," and included directions for making a static machine, and for electroplating door-keys. He later abandoned the sciences for the postal service, and is now, I believe, retired. "Boys' Useful Pastimes," and my apparent interest in it, may have been responsible for my father's decision to transfer me from F. Knapp's Institute to the Baltimore Polytechnic in 1892. If so, it did me an evil service in the end, for my native incapacity for mechanics made my studies at the Polytechnic a sheer waste of time, though I managed somehow to pass the examinations, even in such abysmal subjects as steam engineering.

The influence of "Huck Finn" was immensely more powerful and durable. It not only reinforced my native aversion to the common run of boys' books; it also set me upon a systematic exploration of all the volumes in the old secretary, and before I finished with them I had looked into every one of them, including even Brother Schultz's sombre history of Freemasonry in Maryland. How many were actually intelligible to a boy of eight, nine, ten? I should say about a fourth. I managed to get through most of Dickens, but only by dint of hard labor, and it was not until I discovered Thackeray, at fourteen, that the English novel really began to lift me. George Eliot floored me as effectively as a text in Hittite, and to the present day I have never read "Adam Bede" or "Daniel Deronda" or "The Mill on the Floss," or developed any desire to do so. So far as I am concerned, they will remain mere names to the end of the chapter, and as hollow and insignificant as the names of Gog and Magog.

But I plowed through Chambers' Encyclopedia relentlessly, beginning with the shortest articles and gradually working my way into the longer ones. The kitchen-midden of irrelevant and incredible information that still burdens me had its origins in those pages, and I almost wore them out acquiring it. I read, too, the whole of Lossing, nearly all of Charlotte M. Yonge, and even some of Duyckinck, perhaps the dullest historian ever catalogued by faunal naturalists on this or any other earth. My brother Charlie and I enjoyed "Our Living World" chiefly because of the colored pictures, but I also read long stretches of it, and astonished my father by calling off the names of nearly all the wild beasts when the circus visited Baltimore in 1889. Finally, I recall reading both "Life Among the Mormons" and "One Thousand Proofs That the Earth Is Not a Globe."

Thus launched upon the career of a bookworm, I presently began to reach out right and left for more fodder. When the Enoch Pratt Free Library of Baltimore opened a branch in Hollins street, in March, 1886, I was still a shade too young to be excited, but I had a card before I was nine, and began an almost daily harrying of the virgins at the delivery desk. In 1888 my father subscribed to *Once-a-Week,* the predecessor of *Collier's,* and a little while later there began to come with it a long series of cheap reprints of contemporary classics, running from Tennyson's poems to Justin M'Carthy's "History of Our Own Times"; and simultaneously there appeared from parts unknown a similar series of cheap reprints of scientific papers, including some of Herbert Spencer. I read them all, sometimes with shivers of puzzlement and sometimes with delight, but always calling for more. I began to inhabit a world that was two-thirds letterpress and only one-third trees, fields, streets and people. I acquired round shoulders, spindly shanks, and a despondent view of humanity. I read everything that I could find in English, taking in some of it but boggling most of it.

This madness ran on until I reached adolescence, and began to distinguish between one necktie and another, and to notice the curiously divergent shapes, dispositions and aromas of girls. Then, gradually, I began to let up.

But to this day I am still what might be called a reader, and have a high regard for authors.

IRVIN S. COBB

A Plea for Old Cap Collier

"I refer, my son, to a book called Huckleberry
Finn. . . ."

For a good many years now I
have been carrying this idea round with me. It was more or less
of a loose and unformed idea, and it wouldn't jell. What brought
it round to the solidification point was this: Here the other week,
being half sick, I was laid up over Sunday in a small hotel in a
small seacoast town. I had read all the newspapers and all the
magazines I could get hold of. The local bookstore, of course, was
closed. They won't let the oysters stay open on Sunday in that
town. The only literature my fellow guests seemed interested
in was mail-order tabs and price currents.

Finally, when despair was about to claim me for her own, I ran
across an ancient Fifth Reader, all tattered and stained and having
that smell of age which is common to old books and old sheep.
I took it up to bed with me, and I read it through from cover to
cover. Long before I was through the very idea which for so
long had been sloshing round inside of my head—this idea which,
as one might say, had been aged in the wood—took shape. Then
and there I decided that the very first chance I had I would sit
me down and write a plea for Old Cap Collier.

In my youth I was spanked freely and frequently for doing

many different things that were forbidden, and also for doing the same thing many different times and getting caught doing it. That, of course, was before the Boy Scout movement had come along to show how easily and how sanely a boy's natural restlessness and a boy's natural love for adventure may be directed into helpful channels; that was when nearly everything a normal, active boy craved to do was wrong and, therefore, held to be a spankable offense.

This was a general rule in our town. It did not especially apply to any particular household, but it applied practically to all the households with which I was in any way familiar. It was a community where an old-fashioned brand of applied theology was most strictly applied. Heaven was a place which went unanimously Democratic every fall, because all the Republicans had gone elsewhere. Hell was a place full of red-hot coals and clinkered sinners and unbaptized babies and a smell like somebody cooking ham, with a deputy devil coming in of a morning with an asbestos napkin draped over his arm and flicking a fireproof cockroach off the table cloth and leaning across the back of Satan's chair and saying: "Good mornin', boss. How're you going to have your lost souls this mornin'—fried on one side or turned over?"

Sunday was three weeks long, and longer than that if it rained. About all a fellow could do after he'd come back from Sunday school was to sit round with his feet cramped into the shoes and stockings which he never wore on week days and with the rest of him incased in starchy, uncomfortable dress-up clothes—just sit round and sit round and itch. You couldn't scratch hard either. It was sinful to scratch audibly and with good, broad, free strokes, which is the only satisfactory way to scratch. In our town they didn't spend Sunday; they kept the Sabbath, which is a very different thing.

Looking back on my juvenile years it seems to me that, generally speaking, when spanked I deserved it. But always there were two punishable things against which—being disciplined—my youthful spirit revolted with a sort of inarticulate sense of injustice. One was for violation of the Sunday code, which struck me as wrong—the code, I mean, not the violation—without knowing exactly why it was wrong; and the other, repeated times without number, was when I had been caught reading *nickul libruries,* erroneously referred to by our elders as dime novels.

I read them at every chance; so did every normal boy of my acquaintance. We traded lesser treasures for them; we swapped them on the basis of two old volumes for one new one; we maintained a clandestine circulating-library system which had its branch offices in every stable loft in our part of town. The more daring among us read them in school behind the shelter of an open geography propped up on the desk.

Shall you ever forget the horror of the moment when, carried away on the wings of adventure with Nick Carter or Big-Foot Wallace or Frank Reade or bully Old Cap, you forgot to flash occasional glances of cautious inquiry forward in order to make sure the teacher was where she properly should be, at her desk up in front, and read on and on until that subtle sixth sense which comes to you when a lot of people begin staring at you warned you something was amiss, and you looked up and round you and found yourself all surrounded by a ring of cruel, gloating eyes?

I say cruel advisedly, because up to a certain age children are naturally more cruel than tigers. Civilization has provided them with tools, as it were, for practicing cruelty, whereas the tiger must rely only on his teeth and his bare claws. So you looked round, feeling that the shadow of an impending doom encompassed you, and then you realized that for no telling how long the teacher had been standing just behind you, reading over your shoulder.

And at home were you caught in the act of reading them, or—what from the parental standpoint was almost as bad—in the act of harboring them? I was. Housecleaning times, when they found them hidden under furniture or tucked away on the back shelves of pantry closets, I was paddled until I had the feelings of a slice of hot buttered toast somewhat scorched on the under side. And each time, having been paddled, I was admonished that boys who read dime novels—only they weren't dime novels at all but cost uniformly five cents a copy—always came to a bad end, growing up to be criminals or Republicans or something equally abhorrent. And I was urged to read books which would help me to shape my career in a proper course. Such books were put into my hands, and I loathed them. I know now why when I grew up my gorge rose and my appetite turned against so-called classics. Their style was so much like the style of the books which older people wanted me to read when I was in my early teens.

Such were the specious statements advanced by the oldsters. And we had no reply for their argument, or if we had one could not find the language in which to couch it. Besides there was another and a deeper reason. A boy, being what he is, the most sensitive and the most secretive of living creatures regarding his innermost emotions, rarely does bare his real thoughts to his elders, for they, alas, are not young enough to have a fellow feeling, and they are too old and they know too much to be really wise.

What we might have answered, had we had the verbal facility and had we not feared further painful corporeal measures for talking back—or what was worse, ridicule—was that reading Old Cap Collier never yet sent a boy to a bad end. I never heard of a boy who ran away from home and really made a go of it who was actuated at the start by the *nickul librury*. Burning with a sense of injustice, filled up with the realization that we were not appreciated at home, we often talked of running away and going out West to fight Indians, but we never did. I remember once two of us started for the Far West, and got nearly as far as Oak Grove Cemetery, when—the dusk of evening impending—we decided to turn back and give our parents just one more chance to understand us.

What, also, we might have pointed out was that in a five-cent story the villain was absolutely sure of receiving suitable and adequate punishment for his misdeeds. Right then and there, on the spot, he got his. And the heroine was always so pluperfectly pure. And the hero always was a hero to his finger tips, never doing anything unmanly or wrong or cowardly, and always using the most respectful language in the presence of the opposite sex. There was never any sex problem in a *nickul librury*. There were never any smutty words or questionable phrases. If a villain said, "Curse you!" he was going pretty far. Any one of us might whet up our natural instincts for cruelty on Foxe's Book of Martyrs, or read all manner of unmentionable horrors in the Old Testament, but except surreptitiously we couldn't walk with Nick Carter, whose motives were ever pure and who never used the naughty word even in the passion of the death grapple with the top-booted forces of sinister evil.

We might have told our parents, had we had the words in which to state the case and they but the patience to listen, that in a *nickul librury* there was logic and the thrill of swift action and the sharp spice of adventure. There, invariably virtue was rewarded and villainy confounded; there, inevitably was the final triumph for law and for justice and for the right; there, embalmed in one thin paper volume, was all that Sanford and Merton lacked; all that the Rollo books never had. We might have told them that though the Leatherstocking Tales and Robin-

187

son Crusoe and Two Years Before the Mast and Ivanhoe were all well enough in their way, the trouble with them was that they mainly were so long-winded. It took so much time to get to where the first punch was, whereas Ned Buntline or Col. Prentiss Ingraham would hand you an exciting jolt on the very first page, and sometimes in the very first paragraph.

You take J. Fenimore Cooper now. He meant well and he had ideas, but his Indians were so everlastingly slow about getting under way with their scalping operations! Chapter after chapter there was so much fashionable and difficult language that the plot was smothered. You couldn't see the woods for the trees.

But it was the accidental finding of an ancient and reminiscent volume one Sunday in a little hotel which gave me the cue to what really made us such confirmed rebels against constituted authority, in a literary way of speaking. The thing which inspired us with hatred for the so-called juvenile classic was a thing which struck deeper even than the sentiments I have been trying to describe.

The basic reason, the underlying motive, lay in the fact that in the schoolbooks of our adolescence, and notably in the school readers, our young mentalities were fed forcibly on a pap which affronted our intelligence at the same time that it cloyed our adolescent palates. It was not altogether the lack of action; it was more the lack of plain common sense in the literary spoon victuals which they ladled into us at school that caused our youthful souls to revolt. In the final analysis it was this more than any other cause which sent us up to the haymow for delicious, forbidden hours in the company of Calamity Jane and Wild Bill Hickok.

Midway of the old dog-eared reader which I picked up that day I came across a typical example of the sort of stuff I mean. I hadn't seen it before in twenty-five years; but now, seeing it, I remembered it as clearly almost as though it had been the week before instead of a quarter of a century before when for the first time it had been brought to my attention. It was a piece entitled The Shipwreck, and it began as follows:

> In the winter of 1824 Lieutenant G——, of the United States Navy, with his beautiful wife and child, embarked in a packet at Norfolk bound to South Carolina.

So far so good. At least, here is a direct beginning. A family group is going somewhere. There is an implied promise that before they have traveled very far something of interest to the reader will happen to them. Sure enough, the packet runs into a storm and founders. As she is going down Lieutenant G—— puts his wife and baby into a lifeboat manned by sailors, and then— there being no room for him in the lifeboat—he remains behind upon the deck of the sinking vessel, while the lifeboat puts off for shore. A giant wave overturns the burdened cockleshell and he sees its passengers engulfed in the waters. Up to this point the chronicle has been what a chronicle should be. Perhaps the phraseology has been a trifle toploftical, and there are a few words in it long enough to run as serials, yet at any rate we are getting an effect in drama. But bear with me while I quote the next paragraph, just as I copied it down:

> The wretched husband saw but too distinctly the destruction of all he held dear. But here alas and forever were shut off from him all sublunary prospects. He fell upon the deck —powerless, senseless, a corpse—the victim of a sublime sensibility!

There's language for you! How different it is from that historic passage when the crack of Little Sure Shot's rifle rang out and another Redskin bit the dust. Nothing is said there about anybody having his sublunary prospects shut off; nothing about the Redskin becoming the victim of a sublime sensibility. In fifteen graphic words and in one sentence Little Sure Shot croaked him, and then with bated breath you moved on to the next paragraph, sure of finding in it yet more attractive casualties snappily narrated.

No, sir! In the *nickul librury* the author did not waste his time and yours telling you that an individual on becoming a corpse would simultaneously become powerless and senseless. He credited your intelligence for something. For contrast, take the immortal work entitled Deadwood Dick of Deadwood, or, The Picked Party, by Edward L. Wheeler, a copy of which has just come to my attention again nearly thirty years after the time of my first reading of it. Consider the opening paragraph:

> The sun was just kissing the mountain tops that frowned down upon Billy-Goat Gulch, and in the aforesaid mighty seam in the face of mighty Nature the shadows of a warm June night were gathering rapidly.
>
> The birds had mostly hushed their songs and flown to their nests in the dismal lonely pines, and only the tuneful twang of a well-played banjo aroused the brooding quiet, save it be the shrill, croaking screams of a crow, perched upon the top of a dead pine, which rose from the nearly perpendicular mountain side that retreated in the ascending from the gulch bottom.

That, as I recall, was a powerfully long bit of description for a *nickul librury,* and having got it out of his system Mr. Wheeler wasted no more valuable space on the scenery. From this point on he gave you action—action with reason behind it and logic to it and the guaranty of a proper climax and a satisfactory conclusion to follow. Deadwood Dick marched many a flower-strewn mile through my young life, but to the best of my recollection he never shut off anybody's sublunary prospects. If a party deserved killing Deadwood just naturally up and killed him, and the historian told about it in graphic yet straightforward terms of speech; and that was all there was to it, and that was all there should have been to it.

At the risk of being termed an iconoclast and a smasher of the pure high ideals of the olden days, I propose to undertake to show that practically all of the preposterous asses and the impossible idiots of literature found their way into the school readers of my generation. With the passage of years there may have been some reform in this direction, but I dare affirm, without having positive knowledge of the facts, that a majority of these half-wits still are being featured in the grammar-grade literature of the present time. The authors of school readers, even in modern school readers, surely are no smarter than the run of grown-ups even, say, as you and as I; and we blindly go on holding up as examples before the eyes of the young of the period the characters and the acts of certain popular figures of poetry and prose who— did but we give them the acid test of reason—would reveal themselves either as incurable idiots, or else as figures in scenes and incidents which physically could never have occurred.

You remember, don't you, the schoolbook classic of the noble lad who by reason of his neat dress, and by his use in the most casual conversation of the sort of language which the late Mr. Henry James used when he was writing his very Jamesiest, secured a job as a trusted messenger in the large city store or in the city's large store, if we are going to be purists about it, as the boy in question undoubtedly was?

It seems that he had supported his widowed mother and a large family of brothers and sisters by shoveling snow and, I think, laying brick or something of that technical nature. After this lapse of years I won't be sure about the brick-laying, but at any rate, work was slack in his regular line, and so he went to the proprietor of this vast retail establishment and procured a responsible position on the strength of his easy and graceful personal address and his employment of some of the most stylish adjectives in the dictionary. At this time he was nearly seven years old—yes, sir, actually nearly seven. We have the word of the schoolbook for it. We should have a second chapter on this boy. Probably at nine he was being considered for president of Yale —no, Harvard. He would know too much to be president of Yale.

Then there was the familiar instance of the Spartan youth who having stolen a fox and hidden it inside his robe calmly stood up and let the animal gnaw his vitals rather than be caught with it in his possession. But, why? I ask you, why? What was the good of it all? What object was served? To begin with, the boy had absconded with somebody else's fox, or with somebody's else fox, which is undoubtedly the way a compiler of school readers would phrase it. This, right at the beginning, makes the morality of the transaction highly dubious. In the second place, he showed poor taste. If he was going to swipe something, why should he not have swiped a chicken or something else of practical value?

We waive that point, though, and come to the lack of discretion shown by the fox. He starts eating his way out through the boy, a mussy and difficult procedure, when merely by biting an aperture in the tunic he could have emerged by the front way with ease and dispatch. And what is the final upshot of it all? The boy falls dead, with a large unsightly gap in the middle of him. Probably, too, he was a boy whose parents were raising him for their own purposes. As it is, all gnawed up in this fashion and deceased besides, he loses his attractions for everyone except the undertaker. The fox presumably has an attack of acute indigestion. And there you are! Compare the moral of any one of the Old Cap Collier series, where virtue comes into its own and sanity is prevalent throughout and vice gets what it deserves, and all.

In McGuffey's Third Reader, I think it was, occurred that story about the small boy who lived in Holland among the dikes and dams, and one evening he went across the country to carry a few illustrated post cards or some equally suitable gift to a poor blind man, and on his way back home in the twilight he discovered a leak in the sea wall. If he went for help the breach might widen while he was gone and the whole structure give way, and then the sea would come roaring in, carrying death and destruction and windmills and wooden shoes and pineapple cheeses on its crest. At least, this is the inference one gathers from reading Mr. McGuffey's account of the affair.

So what does the quick-witted youngster do? He shoves his little arm in the crevice on the inner side, where already the water is trickling through, thus blocking the leak. All night long he stays there, one small, half-frozen Dutch boy holding back the entire North Atlantic. Not until centuries later, when Judge Alton B. Parker runs for president against Colonel Roosevelt and is defeated practically by acclamation, is there to be presented so historic and so magnificent an example of a contest against tremendous odds. In the morning a peasant, going out to mow the tulip beds, finds the little fellow crouched at the foot of the dike and inquires what ails him. The lad, raising his weary head—but wait, I shall quote the exact language of the book:

"I am hindering the sea from running in," was the simple reply of the child.

Simple? I'll say it is! Positively nothing could be simpler unless it be the stark simplicity of the mind of an author who figures that when the Atlantic Ocean starts boring its way through a crack in a sea wall you can stop it by plugging the hole on the inner side of the sea wall with a small boy's arm. Ned Buntline may never have enjoyed the vogue among parents and teachers that Mr. McGuffey enjoyed, but I'll say this for him—he knew more about the laws of hydraulics than McGuffey ever dreamed.

And there was Peter Hurdle, the ragged lad who engaged in a long but tiresome conversation with the philanthropic and inquisitive Mr. Lenox, during the course of which it developed that Peter didn't want anything. When it came on to storm he got under a tree. When he was hungry he ate a raw turnip. Raw turnips, it would appear, grew all the year round in the fields of the favored land where Peter resided. If the chill winds of autumn blew in through one of the holes in Peter's trousers they blew right out again through another hole. And he didn't care to accept the dime which Mr. Lenox in an excess of generosity offered him, because, it seemed, he already had a dime. When it came to being plumb contented there probably never was a soul on this earth that was the equal of Master Hurdle. He even was satisfied with his name, which I would regard as the ultimate test.

Likewise, there was the case of Hugh Idle and Mr. Toil. Perhaps you recall that moving story? Hugh tries to dodge work; wherever he goes he finds Mr. Toil in one guise or another but always with the same harsh voice and the same frowning eyes, bossing some job in a manner which would cost him his bossship right off the reel in these times when union labor is so touchy. And what is the moral to be drawn from this narrative? I know that all my life I have been trying to get away from work, feeling that I was intended for leisure, though never finding time somehow to take it up seriously. But what was the use of trying to discourage me from this agreeable idea back yonder in the formulative period of my earlier years?

In Harper's Fourth Reader, edition of 1888, I found an article entitled The Difference Between the Plants and Animals. It takes up several pages and includes some of the fanciest language the senior Mr. Harper could disinter from the Unabridged. In my own case—and I think I was no more observant than the average urchin of my age—I can scarcely remember a time when I could not readily determine certain basic distinctions between such plants and such animals as a child is likely to encounter in the temperate parts of North America.

While emerging from infancy some of my contemporaries may have fallen into the error of the little boy who came into the house with a haunted look in his eye and asked his mother if mulberries had six legs apiece and ran round in the dust of the road, and when she told him that such was not the case with mulberries he said: "Then, mother, I feel that I have made a mistake."

To the best of my recollection, I never made this mistake, or at least if I did I am sure I made no inquiry afterward which might tend further to increase my doubts; and in any event I am sure that by the time I was old enough to stumble over Mr. Harper's favorite big words I was old enough to tell the difference between an ordinary animal—say, a house cat—and any one of the commoner forms of plant life, such as, for example, the scaly-bark hickory tree, practically at a glance. I'll add this too: Nick Carter never wasted any of the golden moments which he and I spent together in elucidating for me the radical points of difference between the plants and the animals.

In the range of poetry selected by the compilers of the readers for my especial benefit as I progressed onward from the primary class into the grammar grades I find on examination of these earlier American authorities an even greater array of chuckle-heads than appear in the prose divisions. I shall pass over the celebrated instance—as read by us in class in a loud tone of voice and without halt for inflection or the taking of breath—of the Turk who at midnight in his guarded tent was dreaming of the hour when Greece her knees in suppliance bent would tremble at his power. I remember how vaguely I used to wonder who it was that was going to grease her knees and why she should feel called upon to have them greased at all. Also, I shall pass over the instance of Abou Ben Adhem, whose name led all the rest in the golden book in which the angel was writing. Why shouldn't it have led all the rest? A man whose front name begins with Ab, whose middle initial is B, and whose last name begins with Ad, will be found leading all the rest in any city directory or any telephone list anywhere. Alphabetically organized as he was, Mr. Adhem just naturally had to lead; and yet for hours on end my teacher consumed her energies and mine in a more or less unsuccessful effort to cause me to memorize the details as set forth by Mr. Leigh Hunt.

In three separate schoolbooks, each the work of a different compilator, I discover Sir Walter Scott's poetic contribution touching on Young Lochinvar—Young Lochinvar who came out of the West, the same as the Plumb plan subsequently came, and the Hiram Johnson presidential boom and the initiative and the referendum and the I. W. W. Even in those ancient times the West appears to have been a favorite place for upsetting things to come from; so I can't take issue with Sir Walter there. But I do take issue with him where he says:

> *So light to the croupe the fair lady he swung,*
> *So light to the saddle before her he sprung!*

Even in childhood's hour I am sure I must have questioned the ability of Young Lochinvar to perform this achievement, for I was born and brought up in a horseback-riding country. Now in the light of yet fuller experience I wish Sir Walter were alive today so I might argue the question out with him.

Let us consider the statement on its physical merits solely. Here we have Young Lochinvar swinging the lady to the croupe, and then he springs to the saddle in front of her. Now to do this he must either take a long running start and leapfrog clear over the lady's head as she sits there, and land accurately in the saddle, which is scarcely a proper thing to do to any lady, aside from the difficulty of springing ten or fifteen feet into the air and coming down, crotched out, on a given spot, or else he must contribute a feat in contortion the like of which has never been duplicated since.

To be brutally frank about it, the thing just naturally is not possible. I don't care if Young Lochinvar was as limber as a string of fresh eels—and he certainly did shake a lithesome calf in the measures of the dance if Sir Walter, in an earlier stanza, is to be credited with veracity. Even so, I deny that he could have done that croupe trick. There isn't a croupier at Monte Carlo who could have done it. Ned Buntline wouldn't have had Buffalo Bill trying to do it. Doug Fairbanks couldn't do it. I couldn't do it myself.

Skipping over Robert Southey's tiresome redundancy in spending so much of his time and mine, when I was in the Fifth-Reader stage, in telling how the waters came down at Ladore when it was a petrified cinch that they, being waters, would have to come down, anyhow, I would next direct your attention to two of the foremost idiots in all the realm of poesy; one a young idiot and one an older idiot, probably with whiskers, but both embalmed in verse, and both, mind you, stuck into every orthodox reader to be glorified before the eyes of childhood. I refer to that juvenile champion among idiots, the boy who stood on the burning deck, and to the ship's captain, in the poem called The Tempest. Let us briefly consider the given facts as regards the latter: It was winter and it was midnight and a storm was on the deep, and the passengers were huddled in the cabin and not a soul would dare to sleep, and they were shuddering there in silence—one gathers the silence was so deep you could hear the shuddering—and the stoutest held his breath, which is considerable feat, as I can testify, because the stouter a fellow gets the harder it is for him to hold his breath for any considerable period of time. Very well, then, this is the condition of affairs. If ever there was a time when those in authority should avoid spreading alarm this was the time. By all the traditions of the maritime service it devolved upon the skipper to remain calm, cool and collected. But what does the poet reveal to a lot of trusting school children?

> *"We are lost!" the captain shouted,*
> *As he staggered down the stair.*

He didn't whisper it; he didn't tell it to a friend in confidence; he bellowed it out at the top of his voice so all the passengers could hear him. The only possible excuse which can be offered for that captain's behavior is that his staggering was due not to the motion of the ship but to alcoholic stimulant. Could you imagine Little Sure Shot, the Terror of the Pawnees, drunk or sober, doing an asinine thing like that? Not in ten thousand years, you couldn't. But then we must remember that Little Sure Shot, being a moral dime-novel hero, never indulged in alcoholic beverages under any circumstances.

The boy who stood on the burning deck has been played up as

an example of youthful heroism for the benefit of the young of our race ever since Mrs. Felicia Dorothea Hemans set him down in black and white. I deny that he was heroic. I insist that he merely was feeble-minded. Let us give this youth the careful once-over: The scene is the Battle of the Nile. The time is August, 1798. When the action of the piece begins the boy stands on the burning deck whence all but him had fled. You see, everyone else aboard had had sense enough to beat it, but he stuck because his father had posted him there. There was no good purpose he might serve by sticking, except to furnish added material for the poetess, but like the leather-headed young imbecile that he was he stood there with his feet getting warmer all the time, while the flame that lit the battle's wreck shone round him o'er the dead. After which:

> *There came a burst of thunder sound;*
> *The boy—oh! where was he?*
> *Ask of the winds, that far around*
> *With fragments strewed the sea—*

Ask the winds. Ask the fragments. Ask Mrs. Hemans. Or, to save time, inquire of me.

He has become totally extinct. He is no more and he never was very much. Still we need not worry. Mentally he must have been from the very outset a liability rather than an asset. Had he lived, undoubtedly he would have wound up in a home for the feeble-minded. It is better so, as it is—better that he should be spread about over the surface of the ocean in a broad general way, thus saving all the expense and trouble of gathering him up and burying him and putting a tombstone over him. He was one of the incurables.

Once upon a time, writing a little piece on another subject, I advanced the claim that the champion half-wit of all poetic anthology was Sweet Alice, who, as described by Mr. English, wept with delight when you gave her a smile, and trembled in fear at your frown. This of course was long before Prohibition came in. These times there are many ready to weep with delight when you offer to give them a smile; but in Mr. English's time and Alice's there were plenty of saloons handy. I remarked, what an awful kill-joy Alice must have been, weeping in a disconcerting manner when somebody smiled in her direction and trembling violently should anybody so much as merely knit his brow.

But when I gave Alice first place in the list I acted too hastily. Second thought should have informed me that undeniably the post of honor belonged to the central figure of Mr. Henry W. Longfellow's poem, Excelsior. I ran across it—Excelsior, I mean—in three different readers the other day when I was compiling some of the data for this treatise. Naturally it would be featured in all three. It wouldn't do to leave Mr. Longfellow's hero out of a volume in which space was given to such lesser village idiots as Casabianca and the Spartan youth. Let us take up this sad case verse by verse:

> *The shades of night were falling fast,*
> *As through an Alpine village passed*
> *A youth, who bore, 'mid snow and ice,*
> *A banner with the strange device,*
> *Excelsior!*

There we get an accurate pen picture of this young man's deplorable state. He is climbing a mountain in the dead of winter. It is made plain later on that he is a stranger in the neighborhood, consequently it is fair to assume that the mountain in question is one he has never climbed before. Nobody hired him to climb any mountain; he isn't climbing it on a bet or because somebody dared him to climb one. He is not dressed for mountain climbing. Apparently he is wearing the costume in which he escaped from the institution where he had been an inmate—a costume consisting simply of low stockings, sandals and a kind of flowing woolen nightshirt, cut short to begin with and badly shrunken in the wash. He has on no rubber boots, no sweater, not even a pair of ear muffs. He also is bare-headed. Well, any time the wearing of hats went out of fashion he could have had no other use for his head, anyhow.

I grant you that in the poem Mr. Longfellow does not go into details regarding the patient's garb. I am going by the illustration in the reader. The original Mr. McGuffey was very strong for illustrations. He stuck them in everywhere in his readers, whether they matched the themes or not. Being as fond of pictures as he undoubtedly was, it seems almost a pity he did not marry the tattooed lady in a circus and then when he got tired of studying her pictorially on one side he could ask her to turn around and let him see what she had to say on the other side. Perhaps he did. I never gleaned much regarding the family history of the Mc-Guffeys.

Be that as it may, the wardrobe is entirely unsuited for the rigors of the climate in Switzerland in winter time. Symptomatically it marks the wearer as a person who is mentally lacking. He needs a keeper almost as badly as he needs some heavy underwear. But this isn't the worst of it. Take the banner. It bears the single word "Excelsior." The youth is going through a strange town late in the evening in his nightie, and it winter time, carrying a banner advertising a shredded wood-fiber commodity which won't be invented until a hundred and fifty years after he is dead!

Can you beat it? You can't even tie it.

Let us look further into the matter:

His brow was sad; his eyes beneath
Flashed like a falchion from its sheath,
And like a silver clarion rung
The accents of that unknown tongue,
"Excelsior!"

Get it, don't you? Even his features fail to jibe. His brow is corrugated with grief, but the flashing of the eye denotes a lack of intellectual coherence which any alienist would diagnose at a glance as evidence of total dementia, even were not confirmatory proof offered by his action in huckstering for a product which doesn't exist, in a language which no one present can understand. The most delirious typhoid fever patient you ever saw would know better than that.

To continue:

In happy homes he saw the light
Of household fires gleam warm and bright;
Above, the spectral glaciers shone,
And from his lips escaped a groan,
"Excelsior!"

The last line gives him away still more completely. He is groaning now, where a moment before he was clarioning. A bit later, with one of those shifts characteristic of the mentally unbalanced, his mood changes and again he is shouting. He's worse than a cuckoo clock, that boy.

"Try not the Pass," the old man said;
"Dark lowers the tempest overhead,
The roaring torrent is deep and wide!"
And loud that clarion voice replied,
"Excelsior!"

"Oh stay," the maiden said, "and rest
Thy weary head upon this breast!"
A tear stood in his bright blue eye,
But still he answered, with a sigh,
"Excelsior!"

"Beware the pine-tree's withered branch!
Beware the awful avalanche!"
This was the peasant's last Good night;
A voice replied, far up the height,
"Excelsior!"

These three verses round out the picture. The venerable citizen warns him against the Pass; pass privileges up that mountain have all been suspended. A kindhearted maiden tenders hospitalities of a most generous nature, considering that she never saw the young man before. Some people might even go so far as to say that she should have been ashamed of herself; others, that Mr. Longfellow, in giving her away, was guilty of an indelicacy, to say the least of it. Possibly she was practicing up to quality for membership on the reception committee the next time the visiting firemen came to her town or when there was going to be an Elks' reunion; so I for one shall not question her motives. She was hospitable—let it go at that. The peasant couples with his good-night message a reference to the danger of falling pine wood and also avalanches, which have never been pleasant things to meet up with when one is traveling on a mountain in an opposite direction.

All about him firelights are gleaming, happy families are gathered before the hearthstone, and through the windows the evening yodel may be heard percolating pleasantly. There is every inducement for the youth to drop in and rest his poor, tired, foolish face and hands and thaw out his knee joints and give the maiden a chance to make good on that proposition of hers. But no, high up above timber line he has an engagement with himself and Mr. Longfellow to be frozen as stiff as a dried herring; and so, now groaning, now with his eyes flashing, now with a tear—undoubtedly a frozen tear—standing in the eye, now clarioning, now sighing, onward and upward he goes:

> *At break of day, as heavenward*
> *The pious monks of Saint Bernard*
> *Uttered the oft-repeated prayer,*
> *A voice cried through the startled air,*
> *"Excelsior!"*

I'll say this much for him: He certainly is hard to kill. He can stay out all night in those clothes, with the thermometer below zero, and at dawn still be able to chirp the only word that is left in his vocabulary. He can't last forever though. There has to be a finish to this lamentable fiasco sometime. We get it:

> *A traveler, by the faithful hound,*
> *Half buried in the snow was found,*
> *Still grasping in his hand of ice*
> *That banner with the strange device,*
> *"Excelsior!"*

> *There in the twilight cold and gray,*
> *Lifeless, but beautiful, he lay,*
> *And from the sky serene and far,*
> *A voice fell, like a falling star,*
> *"Excelsior!"*

The meteoric voice said "Excelsior!" It should have said "Bonehead!" It would have said it, too, if Ned Buntline had been handling the subject, for he had a sense of verities, had Ned.

Probably that was one of the reasons why they barred his works out of all the schoolbooks.

With the passage of years I rather imagine that Lieutenant G——, of the United States Navy, who went to so much trouble and took so many needless pains in order to become a corpse may have vanished from the school readers. I admit I failed to find him in any of the modern editions through which I glanced, but I am able to report, as a result of my researches, that the well-known croupe specialist, Young Lochinvar, is still there, and so likewise is Casabianca, the total loss; and as I said before, I ran across Excelsior three times.

Just here the other day, when I was preparing the material for this little book, I happened upon an advertisement in a New York paper of an auction sale of a collection of so-called dime novels, dating back to the old Beadle's Boy's Library in the early eighties and coming on down through the years into the generation when Nick and Old Cap were succeeding some of the earlier favorites. I read off a few of the leading titles upon the list:

Bronze Jack, the California Thoroughbred; or, The Lost City of the Basaltic Buttes. A strange story of a desperate adventure after fortune in the weird, wild Apache land. By Albert W. Aiken.

Tombstone Dick, the Train Pilot; or, The Traitor's Trail. A story of the Arizona Wilds. By Ned Buntline.

The Tarantula of Taos; or, Giant George's Revenge. A tale of Sardine-box City, Arizona. By Major Sam S. (Buckskin Sam) Hall.

Redtop Rube, the Vigilante Prince; or, The Black Regulators of Arizona. By Major E. L. St. Vrain.

Old Grizzly Adams, the Bear Tamer; or, The Monarch of the Mountains.

Deadly Eye and the Prairie Rover.

Arizona Joe, the Boy Pard of Texas Jack.

Pacific Pete, the Prince of the Revolver.

Kit Carson, King of the Guides.

Leadville Nick, the Boy Sport; or, The Mad Miner's Revenge.

Lighthouse Lige; or, The Firebrand of the Everglades.

The Desperate Dozen; or, The Fair Fiend.

Nighthawk Kit; or, The Daughter of the Ranch.

Joaquin, the Saddle King.

Mustang Sam, the Wild Rider of the Plains.

Adventures of Wild Bill, the Pistol Prince, from Youth to his Death by Assassination. Deeds of Daring, Adventure and Thrilling Incidents in the Life of J. B. Hickok, known to the World as Wild Bill.

These titles and many another did I read, and reading them my mind slid back along a groove in my brain to a certain stable loft in a certain Kentucky town, and I said to myself that if I had a boy—say, about twelve or fourteen years old—I would go to this auction and bid in these books and I would back them up and reënforce them with some of the best of the collected works of Nick Carter and Cap Collier and Nick Carter, Jr., and Frank Reade, and I would buy, if I could find it anywhere, a certain paper-backed volume dealing with the life of the James boys— not Henry and William, but Jesse and Frank—which I read ever so long ago; and I would confer the whole lot of them upon that offspring of mine and I would say to him:

"Here, my son, is something for you; a rare and precious gift. Read these volumes openly. Never mind the crude style in which most of them are written. It can't be any worse than the stilted and artificial style in which your school reader is written; and, anyhow, if you are ever going to be a writer, style is a thing which you laboriously must learn, and then having acquired added wisdom you will forget part of it and chuck the rest of it out of the window and acquire a style of your own, which merely is another way of saying that if you have good taste to start with you will have what is called style in writing, and if you haven't that sense of good taste you won't have a style and nothing can give it to you.

"Read them for the thrills that are in them. Read them, remembering that if this country had not had a pioneer breed of Buckskin Sams and Deadwood Dicks we should have had no native school of dime novelists. Read them for their brisk and stirring movement; for the spirit of outdoor adventure and life which crowds them; for their swift but logical processions of sequences; for the phases of pioneer Americanism they rawly but graphically portray, and for their moral values. Read them along with your Coopers and your Ivanhoe and your Mayne Reids. Read them through, and perhaps some day, if fortune is kinder to you than ever it was to your father, with a background behind you and a vision before you, you may be inspired to sit down and write a dime novel of your own almost good enough to be worthy of mention in the same breath with the two greatest adventure stories—dollar-sized dime novels is what they really are—that ever were written; written, both of them, by sure-enough writing men, who, I'm sure, must have based their moods and their modes upon the memories of the dime novels which they, they in their turn, read when they were boys of your age.

"I refer, my son, to a book called Huckleberry Finn, and to a book called Treasure Island."

A

Sweet Devouring

The pleasures of reading itself—who doesn't remember?—were like those of a Christmas cake, a sweet devouring.

—EUDORA WELTY

ELIZABETH BARRETT BROWNING

Aurora Leigh Discovers Books

Books, books, books!
I had found the secret of a garret room
Piled high with cases in my father's name;
Piled high, packed large,—where, creeping in and out
Among the giant fossils of my past,
Like some small nimble mouse between the ribs
Of a mastodon, I nibbled here and there
At this or that box, pulling through the gap,
In heats of terror, haste, victorious joy,
The first book first. And how I felt it beat
Under my pillow, in the morning's dark,
An hour before the sun would let me read!
My books!
  At last, because the time was ripe,
I chanced upon the poets.

EUDORA WELTY

A Sweet Devouring

I was then nine years old. . . . At that age a child
reads with higher appetite and gratification, and with
those two stars sailing closer together, than ever again
in his growing up.

WHEN I used to ask my mother
which we were, rich or poor, she refused to tell me. I was then
nine years old and of course what I was dying to hear was that
we were poor. I was reading a book called *Five Little Peppers*
and my heart was set on baking a cake for my mother in a stove
with a hole in it. Some version of rich, crusty old Mr. King—up
till that time not living on our street—was sure to come down
the hill in his wheel chair and rescue me if anything went wrong.
But before I could start a cake at all I had to find out if we were
poor, and poor *enough;* and my mother wouldn't tell me, she
said she was too busy. I couldn't wait too long; I had to go on
reading and soon Polly Pepper got into more trouble, some that
was a little harder on her and easier on me.

Trouble, the backbone of literature, was still to me the original
property of the fairy tale, and as long as there was plenty of
trouble for everybody and the rewards for it were falling in the
right spots, reading was all smooth sailing. At that age a child
reads with higher appetite and gratification, and with those two
stars sailing closer together, than ever again in his growing up.

The home shelves had been providing me all along with the usual books, and I read them with love—but snap, I finished them. I read everything just alike—snap. I even came to the *Tales from Maria Edgeworth* and went right ahead, without feeling the bump—then. It *was* noticeable that when her characters suffered she punished them for it, instead of rewarding them as a reader had rather been led to hope. In her stories, the children had to make their choice between being unhappy and good about it and being unhappy and bad about it, and then she helped them to choose wrong. In *The Purple Jar,* it will be remembered, there was the little girl being taken through the shops by her mother and her downfall coming when she chooses to buy something beautiful instead of something necessary. The purple jar, when the shop sends it out, proves to have been purple only so long as it was filled with purple water, and her mother knew it all the time. They don't deliver the water. That's only the cue for stones to start coming through the hole in the victim's worn-out shoe. She bravely agrees she must keep walking on stones until such time as she is offered another choice between the beautiful and the useful. Her father tells her as far as he is concerned she can stay in the house. If I had been at all easy to disappoint, that story would have disappointed me. Of course I did feel what is the good of walking on rocks if they are going to let the water out of the jar too? And it seemed to me that even the illustrator fell down on the characters in that book, not alone Maria Edgeworth, for when a rich, crusty old gentleman gave Simple Susan a guinea for some kind deed she'd done him, there was a picture of the transaction and where was the guinea? I couldn't make out a feather. But I liked *reading* the book all right —except that I finished it.

My mother took me to the Public Library and introduced me: "Let her have any book she wants, except *Elsie Dinsmore*." I looked for the book I couldn't have and it was a row. That was how I learned about the Series Books. The *Five Little Peppers* belonged, so did *The Wizard of Oz,* so did *The Little Colonel,* so did *The Green Fairy Book.* There were many of everything, generations of everybody, instead of one. I wasn't coming to the end of reading, after all—I was saved.

Our library in those days was a big rotunda lined with shelves. A copy of *V. V.'s Eyes* seemed to follow you wherever you went, even after you'd read it. I didn't know what I liked, I just knew what there was a lot of. After *Randy's Spring* there came *Randy's Summer, Randy's Fall* and *Randy's Winter.* True, I didn't care very much myself for her spring, but it didn't occur to me that I might not care for her summer, and then her summer didn't prejudice me against her fall, and I still had hopes as I moved on to her winter. I was disappointed in her whole year as it turned out, but a thing like that didn't keep me from wanting to read every word of it. The pleasures of reading itself—who doesn't remember?—were like those of a Christmas cake, a sweet devouring. The "Randy Books" failed chiefly in being so soon over. Four seasons doesn't make a series.

All that summer I used to put on a second petticoat (our librarian wouldn't let you past the front door if she could see through you), ride my bicycle up the hill and "through the Capitol" (short cut) to the library with my two read books in the basket (two was the limit you could take out at one time when you were a child and also as long as you lived), and tiptoe in ("Silence") and exchange them for two more in two minutes. Selection was no object. I coasted the two new books home, jumped out of my petticoat, read (I suppose I ate and bathed and answered questions put to me), then in all hope put my petticoat back on and rode those two books back to the library to get my next two.

The librarian was the lady in town who wanted to be it. She called me by my full name and said: "Does your mother know where you are? You know good and well the fixed rule of this library: *Nobody is going to come running back here with any book on the same day they took it out.* Get both those things out of here and don't come back till tomorrow. And I can practically see through you."

My great-aunt in Virginia, who understood better about needing more to read than you *could* read, sent me a book so big it had to be read on the floor—a bound volume of six or eight issues of *St. Nicholas* from a previous year. In the very first pages a serial began: *The Lucky Stone* by Abbie Farwell Brown. The illustrations were right down my alley: a heroine so poor she was ragged, a witch with an extremely pointed hat, a rich, crusty old gentleman in—better than a wheel chair—a runaway carriage; and I set to. I gobbled up installment after installment through the whole luxurious book, through the last one, and then came the words, turning me to *un*lucky stone: "To be concluded." The book had come to an end and The Lucky Stone wasn't finished! The witch had it! I couldn't believe this infidelity from my aunt. I still had my secret childhood feeling that if you hunted long enough in a book's pages you could find what you were looking for, and long after I knew books better than that I used to hunt again for the end of *The Lucky Stone.* It never occurred to me that the story had an existence anywhere else outside the pages of that single green-bound book. The last chapter was just something I would have to do without. Polly Pepper could do it. And then suddenly I tried something—I read it again, as much as I had of it. I was in love with books at least partly for what they looked like; I loved the printed page.

In my little circle books were almost never given for Christmas, they cost too much. But the year before I'd been given a book and got a shock. It was from the same classmate who had told me there was no Santa Claus. She gave me a book, all right—*Poems by Another Little Girl*. It looked like a real book, was printed like a real book—but it was *by her*. *Homemade* poems? Illusion-dispelling was her favorite game. She was in such a hurry, she had such a pile to get rid of—her mother's electric runabout was stacked to the bud vases with copies—that she hadn't even time to say, "Merry Christmas!" With only the same raucous laugh with which she had told me, "Been filling my own stocking for years!" she shot me her book, received my Japanese pencil box with a moonlight scene on the lid and a sharpened pencil inside, jumped back into the car and was sped away by her mother. I stood right where they had left me, on the curb in my Little Nurse's uniform, and read that book, and I had no better way to prove when I got through than I had when I started that this was not a real book. But of course it wasn't. The printed page is not absolutely everything.

Then this Christmas was coming, and my grandfather in Ohio sent along in his box of presents an envelope with money in it for me to buy myself the book I wanted.

I went to Kress's. Not everybody knew Kress's sold books, but children just before Christmas know everything Kress's ever sold or will sell. My father had showed us the mirror he was giving my mother to hang above her desk, and Kress's is where my brother and I went to reproduce that by buying a mirror together to give her ourselves, and where our little brother then made us take him and he bought her one his size for fifteen cents. Kress's had also its version of the Series Book, called, exactly like another series, "The Camp Fire Girls," beginning with *The Camp Fire Girls in the Woods*.

I believe they were ten cents each and I had a dollar. But they weren't all that easy to buy, because the series stuck, and to buy some of it was like breaking into a loaf of French bread. Then after you got home, each single book was as hard to open as a box stuck in its varnish, and when it gave way it popped like a firecracker. The covers once prized apart would never close; those books once open stayed open and lay on their backs help-lessly fluttering their leaves like a turned-over June bug. They were as light as a matchbox. They were printed on yellowed paper with corners that crumbled, if you pinched on them too hard, like old graham crackers, and they smelled like attic trunks, caramelized glue, their own confinement with one another and, over all, the Kress's smell—bandanas, peanuts and sandalwood from the incense counter. Even without reading them I loved them. It was hard, that year, that Christmas is a day you can't read.

What could have happened to those books?—but I can tell you about the leading character. His name was Mr. Holmes. He was not a Camp Fire Girl: he wanted to catch one. Through every book of the series he gave chase. He pursued Bessie and Zara—those were the Camp Fire Girls—and kept scooping them up in his touring car, while they just as regularly got away from him. Once Bessie escaped from the second floor of a strange inn by climbing down a gutter pipe. Once she escaped by driving away from Mr. Holmes in his own automobile, which she had learned to drive by watching him. What Mr. Holmes wanted with them —either Bessie or Zara would do—didn't give me pause; I was too young to be a Camp Fire Girl; I was just keeping up. I wasn't alarmed by Mr. Holmes—when I cared for a chill, I knew to go to Dr. Fu Manchu, who had his own series in the library. I wasn't fascinated either. There was one thing I wanted from those books, and that was for me to have ten to read at one blow.

Who in the world wrote those books? I knew all the time they were the false "Camp-Fire Girls" and the ones in the library were the authorized. But book reviewers sometimes say of a book that if anyone else had written it, it might not have been this good, and I found it out as a child—their warning is justified. This was a proven case, although a case of the true not being as good as the false. In the true series the characters were either totally different or missing (Mr. Holmes was missing), and there was too much time given to teamwork. The Kress's Campers, besides getting into a more reliable kind of trouble than the Carnegie Campers, had adventures that even they themselves weren't aware of: the pages were in wrong. There were transposed pages, repeated pages, and whole sections in upside down. There was no way of telling if there was anything missing. But if you knew your way in the woods at all you could enjoy yourself tracking it down. I read the library "Camp Fire Girls," since that's what they were there for, for though they could be read by poorer light they were not as good.

And yet, in a way, the false Campers were no better either. I wonder whether I felt some flaw at the heart of things or whether I was just tired of not having any taste; but it seemed to me when I had finished that the last nine of those books weren't as good as the first one. And the same went for all series books. As long as they are keeping a series going, I was afraid, nothing can really happen. The whole thing is one grand prevention. For my greed, I might have unwittingly dealt with myself in the same way Maria Edgeworth dealt with the one who put her all into the purple jar—I had received word it was just colored water. And my feet hurt too, now and again, from keeping up. That would not have been a good time for me to start in on *Pamela*.

At the Istrione, our movie house, known as the Eye-Strain, stuck in the midst of little girls' "picture-show parties"—we nested in the box—I still enjoyed transposing the Camp Fire Girls into whatever was going on, on the screen. They were in *Drums of*

Jeopardy with Alice Brady and *Always Audacious* with Wallace Reid, and anything else we managed to see. Their role—escaping—fitted in anywhere. What those characters always were was dramatic. Of course, the best thing would have been for them to have had a whole picture to themselves. I wanted Marguerite Clark as Bessie, Mae Marsh as Zara and Theodore Roberts as Mr. Holmes—for, should the conclusion ever come (series books try not to think of that, but I always remembered what a difference in *The Lucky Stone* a conclusion would have made), for they had let him catch them, and then they'd all bounce giggling into one another's arms and the picture could say "The End" and the comedy could start.

And then I found it was nice to come home and read *A Christmas Carol*.

LOUISE DICKINSON RICH

The Little Dickinson Girls

. . . turning us loose in a library was like turning an
alcoholic loose in a wine cellar . . . our minds awhirl
with a heady brew compounded of a few pages of
Tom Paine, a little Pascal . . . or if we happened to
be in the F's, a stout blend of Fielding, Franklin,
Fitzgerald, and Freneau.

OUR ruling passion was books.
I can remember well the day I discovered that I could read. Up to
that time, our parents had read to us. It didn't make any difference what they read. If our father was reading to himself, he
just went on from wherever he was, aloud. We probably didn't
understand a tenth of what was read to us, but some of it stuck,
and we liked to be read to anyhow. We'd sit as still as mice
while the reader's voice went on and on, giving us glimpses of a
fabulous world outside our experience. What we didn't understand we asked about, and if the explanation didn't clear matters up, we pretended that it did, so that the reading would go on.

There was among the books in the parlor a paper-covered
pamphlet with a cover-picture of a man in old-fashioned dress
standing erect and brandishing a sword. The picture intrigued us.
The man was romantically handsome and dashing, and we
wanted to know who he was and what he thought he was doing.

So we bedeviled our father to read us the story, and finally, one Sunday evening, he found time to start it. It was a brief history of the town of Hadley, Massachusetts, up around where we came from, and after a little preliminary bandying about of names and dates, got to the heart of the matter, as far as we were concerned —the story of the man on the cover.

It seemed that two men, named Whalley and Goffe, had taken refuge in Hadley—this was way back before the Revolution—from the officers of the King of England, Charles the Second. Charles was after their hides because they'd been members of the court which sentenced his father, Charles the First, to death. They'd fled to Boston, then to Connecticut, and finally to Hadley, where a minister had hidden them in his cellar for fifteen years. (Here Alice's and my faces started lengthening. Those poor men, cooped up in a cellar all that time! Our father hastily assured us that probably they went out and walked around the country-side at night, looking at the stars and swimming in the river. We felt better, and he went on reading.) One day Indians attacked Hadley, and things looked pretty bad for the settlers, surprised and disorganized. But at the crucial point of the battle a strange man suddenly appeared from nowhere, rallied the white forces to beat off the Indians, and saved the day. It was—

At this point it was seven o'clock and our bedtime, so the book was closed with finality. Our father said he'd finish the story the next evening.

We went to bed and conferred in whispers about the identity of the hero. We were sure that it must be one of the men from the Reverend Russell's cellar, but we wanted the book to tell us so beyond doubt. We couldn't be satisfied until we'd heard it hot from the printed page. The next day I took the pamphlet and turned the leaves, trying by sheer force of wanting to wring from them their secret. It was maddening. The information was there in my hands, but I couldn't get at it. The print on the paper told what I wanted to know, but I couldn't read it. I have never felt so frustrated since in my life.

Then suddenly a word leaped from the page and hit me between the eyes, a stunning blow. It was *regicide,* a word that our father had explained to us the night before. Don't ask me how I knew that those symbols spelled regicide. It sounds unlikely, but it's true. That's what they said, as plainly as though someone had shouted it in my ear. *I could read!* It was the most stirring and revolutionary thing that ever happened to me.

After that, I read all the time. Oh, probably it wasn't as quick as all that, but it seems so now. I was reading quite well when my classmates were still struggling with c-a-t cat, not because I was smarter than they, but simply because I was possessed to read, I guess, and found it the most fascinating occupation in the world. I still do. . . .

The town, it seemed, had allocated a sum of money to be used for cleaning and refurbishing the Public Library. The two librarians, Miss Lucia Christian (Adults) and Miss Rachel Crocker (Children), considered it essential that in addition to the necessary painting and floor finishing, every book in the place should be taken down and dusted.

In those days the shelves were closed to the public. If you wanted a book, you told the librarian about it, and she went and got it for you, while you waited outside the carved wooden fence that separated the sheep from the goats. The shelves came very decidedly under the category of Sacred Ground, available only to the librarians or their duly empowered agents and assistants and jealously guarded from unlawful hands and eyes. There was no random and casual browsing around by the goats, who, if they did nothing worse, could surely be counted upon to put the books back in the wrong places. Under this system some books weren't even touched, let alone read, from one year's end to the next. It wasn't very surprising or unnatural that during that time they collected quite a coating of dust. And who better could be found to cope with the situation than the little Dickinson girls, who in addition to being Reliable, were Readers and Respecters of Books, and who, moreover, could be expected because of their tender years to work for much less than a regular cleaning woman would?

We were paid, I think, five cents an hour, which seemed like the wealth of Croesus to us. By going in right after school, we could make a dime apiece before suppertime; and on Saturday, when we worked in the morning as well as all afternoon, we sometimes amassed as much as thirty-five cents, a truly impressive sum. We liked the money all right, but after the first day or so, we'd have worked for nothing if we'd had to.

We never knew there were so many books in the world. We tried to be honest and conscientious, we tried not to peek, but turning us loose in a library was like turning an alcoholic loose in a wine cellar. We'd open a book with the innocent intention of seeing what it was about, that's all; and fifteen minutes later we'd rouse to find ourselves perched precariously on top of the ladder, or crouched uncomfortably on the floor before a low shelf, or standing like statues in an aisle, devouring page after breathtaking page. We'd slam the book shut and do half the next section at top speed, to make up for lost time. No matter what vows of abstinence we took, sooner or later we'd slip again; and we'd go home in much the same condition as one who has ill-advisedly mixed his drinks, our minds awhirl with a heady brew compounded of a few pages of Tom Paine, a little Pascal, a verse or two of Thomas Love Peacock (What a name!), and a dash of Pepys; or if we happened to be in the F's, a stout blend of Fielding, Franklin, Fitzgerald, and Freneau. It's no wonder that we haven't got really straightened out on some of them yet, especially since we had the bad habit of reading aloud to each other particularly choice gems. It wasn't unusual at all for us to carry home the impression that somewhere in the middle of *The Oregon Trail* was a poem which began, "The world is too much with us; late and soon."

Nevertheless, those five or six weeks of dusting books contributed more to our so-called education than sixteen years, more or less, of school attendance. They gave us, first, some slight comprehension of the vast and varied extent of recorded human knowledge and speculation; but that was the less important contribution. Up to that time, we had accepted, because it never occurred to us to do otherwise, the ready-made set of ideas and attitudes that had been presented to us both at school and at home. We thought that everybody held the same opinions that were handed to us. Now we discovered that such was not the case at all. There were actually some people who didn't think that the Revolution was justified, for example, or that the Patriots —whom we had been led to believe were the finest flower of all that was brave, courteous, kind, and disinterested—were any better than ordinary men, only smarter and luckier. We were shocked and exhilarated. Why, you could believe anything you wanted to! You didn't have to accept what anyone, even teachers, told you!

I suppose that at some time in everyone's life the moment comes when he discovers his own mind and the infinite pleasure of exploring it. I suppose that there is always someone at hand to share this greatest of adventures with you. In my case the occasion happened to be the book dusting and the companion, Alice; and because we were so closely in rapport and saw so much of each other, maybe we traveled faster and further than we would ordinarily have done. We went completely overboard and became iconoclasts of the first order, for a spell there. Eventually we settled down to a middle course of a reasonable skepticism that methodically investigated any new idea before accepting or rejecting it. But it certainly was wonderful while it lasted.

Naturally, we were filled with missionary zeal to impart our discovery of new worlds to others, and events played into our hands. We finally worked ourselves out of our dusting jobs. (And none too soon, I might add. If it had lasted much longer, so violent was our love affair with books, we'd have entirely given up living our own lives in favor of the vicarious living of bookworms. It was a very real danger which we escaped by the skin of our teeth.) But we left the hallowed precincts of the library with our reputations for reliability untarnished.

The following summer, Miss Christian and Miss Crocker were obliged for personal reasons to take their two weeks' vacations at the same time. Usually they took turns, one going away to relax while the other held the fort and kept an eye on the substitute librarian, whoever she might be. Faced with the necessity of leaving their sacred trust in untested hands, they thought of the little Dickinson girls, who although rather young for the posts, were fabulously Reliable. (Yes, honestly! I, too, find it hard to believe now.) So we were approached and snapped at the chance. We went into the library for a week or so to learn the ropes; and then Miss Christian and Miss Crocker took off, leaving us in charge. If they were troubled with misgivings, they were too tactful to say so . . . they knew we understood the regular library procedure well enough for practical purposes; and probably they thought we couldn't do much damage anyhow in two short weeks.

That's where they underestimated us. Oh, we fulfilled our technical obligations meticulously, stamping dates on charge slips with a firm flourish, sending out overdue notices on the dot, keeping at bay those members of the public who thought this would be a good chance to prowl around in the stacks, frowning at anyone who raised his voice above the lawful whisper, collecting and recording fines with the impersonal severity of cops, and shelving books with a care bordering on fussiness. No one could find basis for complaint about us on any of those scores. It was in the less easily defined realm of the cultural that we went haywire.

We decided with the arrogance of which only the psychotic or the very young and immature are capable that we would give people not what they wanted to read, but what we thought they ought, for their own good, to have. We constituted ourselves into a sort of drumhead court to hand down quick, summary, and unalterable decisions on what was wrong with various individuals and what they'd better be given to read to correct their deficiencies. Miss Babson? She wants a nice little love story? She's much too silly already. It's time she stopped thinking about moonlight and roses. (Miss Babson was incredibly old, all of thirty; it was a wonder to us that she could still get around without a wheelchair.) Let's give her *Lives of the Great Philosophers*. Mrs. Hilton, that old calamity howler? She gets *Pollyanna*. That ought to straighten her out. The mathematics teacher at the Normal School? But it's his vacation! He *can't* want Bowditch's *Practical Navigator*. He's supposed to be resting his brains. Give him a good Jack London.

We had visions of completely revolutionizing the reading habits of the town, and through the medium of the printed page, bringing about a modern Utopia. We were sure that given time, our reformation would work. Time, fortunately—since if we'd been granted it, we'd undoubtedly have reduced Miss Christian's cherished Circulation to Absolute Zero—was what we didn't have. At the end of the two weeks, we retired to private life, and our victims went thankfully back to their former reading habits. Deprived of our Mission, we moped around for a few days; but then something else came up to absorb our energies. That was one nice thing about being so very young; no matter what our failures might be, we were conscious of the fact that we were going to live forever to correct them.

G. B. STERN

Another Part of the Forest

"Don't touch, child. . . ." You smiled seraphically;
you had already touched, and proved it for yourself.

A LONDON child of the past, prob-
ably also a Brighton child or a Birmingham child, always accepted
railings as a matter of course, created as part of a seven-day universe; plenty of juvenile uses for railings; but chiefly for that
urchin impulse to run along drawing a hoopstick across them,
making sweet music. . . .

Usually, in spring, when the awnings went up and the window-
boxes blossomed, the railings became a freshly painted menace,
vivid and sticky and very, very beautiful. "Don't touch, child,
they're wet!" You smiled seraphically; you had already touched,
and proved it for yourself.

Your parents had a garden with walls, but how much more
fascinating were those little private squares, exclusive to the
residents who lived in the houses on four sides; and how lucky,
how happy was your friend whose discriminating parents had
chosen to live in one of these houses, with a special key to the
square guarded by iron railings!

But today we must put away childish things; put away our
hoopsticks and toy balloons. Children of the future may find
funny problems set for them in their arithmetic books: If three

men and a boy can pull up 240 yards of railings in four days, and assuming that a boy and a half equals one man, how long would it take one man and five boys to pull up 17,542 yards? And not seeing those phantom battleships, they will look on it as just another beastly sum, with no more emotion than we in our youth looked on those three men and a boy who were eternally papering walls at so much per square yard. Yet for us today, Lewis Carroll has materialised into sober sense, and we are not derided for asking how many aluminum saucepans go to make a tea-tray in the sky . . .

It is odd that between the ages of eight and twelve I should have been capable of reading Ouida and Mrs. Molesworth with equal abandon. I gather that neo-Georgian juvenile fiction still has a strong flavour of Edward Lear, Lewis Carroll and G. E. Farrow; nonsense books, in fact, but with a strong zoological or aeronautic flavouring. Nonsense books with nonsense words must always be popular. Standing on my Adam mantelpiece was a little blue and silver tree, less than two feet high, a present from John van Druten. It arrived in an enormous wooden case from New York; they could hardly get it up the seventy-two stairs; within the outer box it was encased in so many inner boxes and wrappings that I expected ultimately a pea or at best a walnut lying breathless in cotton-wool. That tree bore a strange fruit which at once I recognised as gombobbles. "This is a gombobble tree!" I said, nonchalantly botanical. It was only when I discovered that nobody knew what I meant except those who in their youth had read the Wallypug books, that I realised gombobble is not what is known as a dictionary word. "Chortle," on the other hand, has, I believe, found its way into the dictionary: "O frabjous day! Callooh! Callay! He chortled in his joy!"

At this point of my reflections I heard a child in the next garden give a joyous chortle which inevitably means a practical joke successfully brought off, and which means equally that someone else, probably a grown-up, is *not* chortling.

My special camping-place for reading, as a child, was uncomfortably crouched on the floor at the foot of the forbidden shelves in the dining-room. There with a loud Ave, an ecstatic Salve and a woebegone Vale, I discovered "Jane Eyre." In those days reading was to me a wild abandon, whereas now it is, more often than not, a sober though unbreakable habit. As an extenuating circumstance I must plead that I was never that sort of wistful infant who spent hour after hour lying face downwards on the hearthrug, which seems to have been practically the only position in which Grand Old Men could absorb literature during their limber boyhood; eagerly lapping up Gibbon and Carlyle and, in gauzier moments, the "Morte d'Arthur." Children in books always do their reading either prone on the hearthrug, or, should hearthrug be lacking, astride of the fork of an old apple tree. When the old apple tree, too, is lacking, I suppose they sit in a chair like the rest of us.

At the foot of the dining-room bookcase, then, I also read "Vice Versa," "Vanity Fair," and all the Works, I use the capital with deliberate solemnity, and repeat it, all the Works of Bulwer Lytton. . . . "Harold" and "The Last Days of Pompeii" were even from a parent's point of view perfectly suitable because they were "historical"; the matter was far otherwise when I eagerly laid hold of "Night and Morning" and "Ernest Maltravers" and "The Two Gentlemen of Verona," who were not nice gentlemen at all. Naturally I was interested in the books my parents read and talked about during my childhood; it must have seemed to me necessary to look at every one of them myself, to make sure it was all right for them. "The Marriage of William Ashe" by Mrs. Humphry Ward got rather confused in my mind with "Lady

Adelaide" by Mrs. Henry Wood and "Lady Audley's Secret" by
Miss Braddon. And a book called "A Marriage of Convenience,"
translated from the French, somehow found its way onto my
nursery bookshelves: I have never known why; stricter super-
vision would hastily have whipped it out and carried it downstairs again and locked it up. At one period, Mother and Father
talked in low murmurs about Oscar Wilde's "De Profundis";
so low were the murmurs that I was sure it must be an entrancing
story; years later I bought a pirated paper copy in the street for
twopence, and bound it in chintz. I wonder why I bound it in
chintz? "The Green Carnation" amused me, though I had not
realised it was a parody by a brilliant young man called Robert
Hitchens, and read it entranced as a straight-forward narrative.
Henry Seton Merriman was popular then, and it was a joke of the
early nineteen hundreds to refer to "Barlasch of the Guard" as
"Eyelash of the Guard." And "Elizabeth and Her German
Garden" and "The Solitary Summer." When the author of these,
five years ago, took me for a delightful picnic in the snow in the
South of France (they are so seldom all together, the snow and
the South and Elizabeth, that I felt I was one up on Browning),
I was suddenly able to disconcert her with long quotations from
her first novels about a similar picnic by the frozen Baltic.

Father's favourite novelist was W. J. Locke. "Ah," he used to
say to me, not unkindly but in all sincerity, long after I had
started writing. "When you can write like Locke, *then* you'll be
worth reading." Idolising my father, I did my best to please him;
and managed, I think, in my first two or three books, to imitate
a great deal of Locke's whimsicality, though not his peculiar
charm. Many years later, when I stayed in the South of France,
I was able to hobnob quite happily with Wells, Maugham, Aldous
Huxley and P. G. Wodehouse, and while certainly not fit to
black their boots I still did not see why I should not sit down to

table with them; but my father's influence was still so strong after his death that, though I knew W. J. Locke also lived somewhere in the neighbourhood, awe and reverence would not allow me to seek personal contact. He died, and I mourned for him as my father would have mourned. . . .

The Apocrypha and "The Swiss Family Robinson" (I swear the link is accidental) also belong vividly to my childhood; then came a bewildered transition stage from Lamb's "Tales of Shakespeare" to the dramatist unexpurgated, when I wondered which had gone wrong in the story, Shakespeare or Charles-and-Mary? And Kingsley's "Heroes" accompanied by Charles Robinson's swirling illustrations to make Perseus and Jason even more attractive. I lost a dollar once to Mr. Somerset Maugham over whether or not Perseus arrived on Pegasus to rescue Andromeda. My memory of the picture in "Heroes" showed him transported by the Sandals of swiftness lent by Hermes to Pallas Athene, and passed on to Perseus without asking (a most reprehensible action). As the argument sprang up in the train between New York and South Carolina, we had to wait for settlement till we arrived at Mr. Nelson Doubleday's home; there the Classical Dictionary ignored my Kingsley and gave cold judgment in favour of Mr. Maugham, who unchivalrously pocketed the dollar.

When I was a child, two weekly journals came regularly to our house, both now defunct: *Black and White* and the *Ladies' Pictorial.* I looked on these as mine before they were Mother's, especially the *Ladies' Pictorial* which had a Children's Page and competitions. (And what could Mother want with all those fashion pictures? she who already had a wardrobe almost approaching Queen Elizabeth's famous three hundred and sixty-five dresses and begin fresh the next year?) My prize in a competition was a bound volume of the *Sunday at Home,* with a serial called "In the Days of Calvin," about Geneva and a boy called Norbert de Caulaincourt who was Calvin's ardent young disciple. Thanks to this, I am still, whenever Calvin is mentioned, less vague in my history than usual; though my conceit has been somewhat tempered by a piece of information from my young secretary, not five minutes ago, that he often preached on right drainage and the extermination of rats. A story in Kipling's "Rewards and Fairies" is also deeply knowledgeable about the extermination of rats as a cause of plague. How much more often are wise men practical than is usually acknowledged! So-called practical men (like Mr. Wilcox in "Howard's End") enjoy pretending in a burly robust style that genius must be helpless until the plumber comes, cheery and late. Mark Twain's "The Prince and the Pauper," I read eagerly before I had any doubt that everything in print must be true. It related with gusto how the first few weeks of the reign of the boy king Edward VI were just a bit tumbled and funny because he had changed places with a gutter-urchin who resembled him and they could not get a chance to change back in time for little Edward the impostor to say in which drawer he had slung the Great Seal after he had cracked nuts with it. I thought then, puzzled, only of seals that were alive, and did not know that the Great Seal is so important that because of it and to this day the Lord Chancellor is not allowed to leave the country during office ("Here, old man, hold this for me for a fortnight while I run across to the Engadine; only don't put it down even during lunch because you've got to feel Trimmensely Responsible").

While still in my late teens, I was asked to supply a story for a juvenile Patriotic Reader. "Patches of Red," I called it; and it was all about a little Boer boy who was sent to school in England and learnt that all patches of red were British territory, and fought for England against the Boers in 1900, and was wounded and bled for England—you perceive the big thrill which so subtly stressed the title twice—and recovered and married an English girl and lived happily ever after. I hope it did no lasting harm to the children who were led to browse on Readers. For they do leave traces, as lasting as those out of juvenile historical fiction; I read all about the Dead Sea in one of them when I was probably about eight, and in consequence scraps of information about the Dead Sea still occupy suburbs of my brain, together with bits about Calvin and Edward VI, and bits from "Before Antwerp" by Evelyn Everett Green; a fascinating account of a Flemish family of youngsters in Antwerp—with the usual English cousin thrown in to make it all seem better—during its siege by the Spanish Prince of Parma. "Days of Bruce," by Grace Aguilar, cleared up obscure Scottish history even before I came to Scott; and "The Oak Staircase" still makes it impossible for me to drive through Taunton without imagining the school where the Maids of Taunton worshipped the handsome Duke of Monmouth and embroidered for him a banner in blue and gold, and suffered for it when cruel Judge Jeffreys came to the town to hold his Assizes after the Rebellion. That was, I am sure, a well-written and vivid story, though ungratefully I forget the author's name; the heroine married a boy of fourteen when she was twelve, and only afterwards was sent to school; I was myself a schoolgirl when I read it, shielded by the lid of a desk during the history class when a Weak mistress had replaced a Strong mistress. Perhaps (I reflected in a rather bothered way), perhaps I ought to be thinking of getting married. I should not have been such a fool had not my father frequently reminded me that in the Orient girls got married before they were—well, whatever age I happened to be whenever he said it. Then he would burst into a shout of laughter at my guilty expression; but even then I was not wholly reassured, and I thought it hard that when I *did* get engaged (for three days) at the age of sixteen Father suddenly deserted the Orient idea, and went about twinkling and blowing out his cheeks and calling, "Where's the bride?" All very well, but it was only to please him that I had accepted the offer.

It is exasperating, the way that almost every historical book one reads as a child, when nowadays recalled, seems to be an ironic comment on our present somewhat overdone privilege of being alive to witness the making of history. One of my very favourite books was the Dutch classic for children, "Hans Brinker, or the Silver Skates." From this fascinating tale I absorbed like pills in jam a first-class education in the customs of Holland, the geography of Holland, the history, art and literature of Holland, and, most useful of all, perhaps, on the typical Dutch outlook as it appeared to that English boy who (of course) was on a visit there to his cousins. I determined then, and went on determining, that I would go to Holland as soon as circumstances made it possible, and would make a frightful scene at every canal corner unless I found all the bits and pieces which the author of "Hans Brinker" had made so familiar; but this happened and that happened and things happened, postponing the trip. I flew over Amsterdam and came down at the aerodrome but merely for lunch, on my way to Denmark, and said to myself, "Next year at tulip-time it *shall* be Holland"; and in 1939, when I had the date fixed, and tulip-time and all the treasures of The Hague and Leyden and Haarlem and Amsterdam and Rotterdam were only a few days beyond my grasp, Mother suddenly collapsed into her last illness.

And in tulip-time of 1940, I did not go either. . . .

PAUL DARCY BOLES

The Vision Then and Now

To a child this time of complete faith in all books seems forever. It has no bounds; it feels infinite, stretching ahead of him the way one summer can be made of millions of years.

SOMETIMES, for a novelist, the stars look very cold about the sky. Then again, something warm and quick happens inside him and the world loosens up; words spring as easily as muscles when a man walks; and the stars are places that are not cold, not aloof, but pleasantly normal and full of awesomeness.

For a long time, when I was a child, wanting to be a novelist from the age of seven, everything that was printed seemed to contain its own breed of magic. It became special just because it was printed. There were, as with a child, no second thoughts and no first critical thoughts. There was a mélange of hearty fare: *Tom Swift* and *Les Misérables,* all in the same gulp; there were *Moby Dick* and *Kazan* and *Baree, Son of Kazan.* All at once there were the novels, then like a rich green world, of Louisa May Alcott. Everything that later seemed prissy and stilted and carefully moralistic was no stumbling block at all: the eye glided over things like that as a fish glides, for the pure joy of being alive in water. The Gary Public Library was a warm expanse with adventure flickering from every shelf; the dark nose-filling smell of old books, old bindings, seemed to reach out with welcome. It seemed to me then that the world was beautifully ordered for reading: dimly, I wondered why more people did not make libraries their headquarters. Snow looked better from a library's windows: when seen above the rim of a book (oh, Doctor Dolittle: oh, your post office, and oh, Polynesia, your parrot!) it seemed to drift down and fill the sills with a rosily cheerful quality, something that partook of the book and the image of the book in the mind. And the shuffling of adults in the distance was nothing but a signal that people were alive in the world which was an extension of, and part of, and indistinguishable from, books. In the long gray dusk when it was time and past time to go home I would still be reading as I went down the library steps and stood teetering on the curb: the great white whale would be out there somewhere in front of me—not far; just as close as the vegetable truck turning the corner and spattering grains of slush over my goloshes. To a child this time of complete faith in all books seems forever. It has no bounds; it feels infinite, stretching ahead of him the way one summer can be made of millions of years.

This vision of the full life, of mankind as part of books and the novel as part of man's life, began burning early and it has never really gone out. I can still go back and recapture the enormous feeling of discovery which came with the first knowledge of reading: I can remember the book (in fact, I still have it somewhere, and a very slight aura of magic still stays around it, though it is dull reading) which would be mine, with my name written carefully on the flyleaf, as soon as I could read it aloud. Its title was *Father Thrift and His Animal Friends*. I was five, then, and it is not the story so much as the sensation of giant doors opening which sight of the dark green cover and the bright illustrations brings back now, like the smell of certain perfume evoking the thought of a lovely girl you once knew.

I was lucky in that, at home, few restrictions were placed on what I read. I remember that one summer night, my grandmother, inspired by some editorial in an educational journal (I have a notion it was the old *Literary Digest*) put a clamp on the works of Mr. Edgar Rice Burroughs: No more Tarzan, she said; and, like the Boston public during the bans of Watch and Ward, my curiosity was instantly inflamed and not to be assuaged. Using an Eveready flashlight as reading lamp, I explored Pellucidar and romped with the golden lion all night long: in the morning I reflected that it hadn't truly been worth it, and that Kipling, who wasn't banned, really gave you more for your money. These first flickerings of discrimination came and went and came back again; for some reason, inexplicable, some books were better than other books, just as some teachers were better than other teachers, some experiences, not always outwardly more attractive, more lasting and memorable than others.

I think I was lucky too because, at that time, children's reading was not viewed with quite the owlish and efficient solemnity it is now: I cannot recall being forced into the narrow valley of works labeled *Children 6 to 9,* or *Ages 10–12.* I was a hound loose in a world of rich scents and magnificently interlaced trails; if after a hard hunt I brought home nothing but a rabbit, it made no difference; there was God's plenty to seek and find, and chances were good that next day I would pick up the reek of a mountain lion. I was also like the pioneer scout free in the limitless forests and grasses of early America, with the same voraciousness, casual waste, and minute-by-minute exaltation at the unrolling of experience, the same impatience with anything that smelled of rules.

That was the boy's vision; and it has not changed too much

today. That is, the early impetus was strong enough so that the feeling is still there; I cannot go into any library, private or public, without a sensation of immense revelations about to be made. I cannot sit down in front of a thousand sheets of paper to begin writing a novel without the same excited, tremendous feeling: an emotion that is like stout Cortez's men, staring at each other with a wild surmise. All the potential gold of the earth seems to be about to reveal itself to me; all the massive secrets of mankind, the unspoken secrets, seem about to speak. The finished work never satisfies me; an hour after I have written the last word of a novel I feel a tapering off of that splendid high mood of discovery which aimed so far and expected so infinitely much and, it seems to me, came up with so little. All the same, in a week, or two weeks, and at most a month, the feeling comes back— it is indescribably strong, and in some ways it is like an explorer who, after spending a little time in civilization, suddenly, over his drink on the cool veranda, remembers the green sweet hot pulse of the jungle, and knows he has to go in there again.

CLIFTON FADIMAN

Portrait of the Author as a Young Reader

> Most children and adolescents know this magical secret
> of concentration, though it is not till they are older
> and duller that they realize it was magical.

THOSE to whom reading is fated
to become important generally shake hands with books early.
But this is not always true. Many distinguished writers were
blockheads at their letters until a comparatively advanced age.
I think, however, of an undistinguished one who was a busy
reader at four: me. My first book was entitled *The Overall Boys*.
The Overall Boys was and doubtless still is a rousing tale of two
devoted brothers, aged five and seven, and their monosyllabic
adventures on a farm. The style was of transparent lucidity. I
found *The Overall Boys* a perfect job then, and, looking back, I
haven't been able to detect any flaws in it. I remember it in greater
detail and certainly with greater pleasure than I do the 576-page
novel I finished yesterday. At four I was convinced that *The
Overall Boys* represented the peak of the art of narrative and
sternly rejected all attempts to make me continue my reading adventures. This resistance endured for a lengthy period—about a
week, I should say. Then I broke down, tried another book, and

have been doing the same sort of thing ever since. But all devout readers will agree that my first literary judgment was correct. Everything after *The Overall Boys* has been anticlimax. One's first book, kiss, home run, is always the best.

Between the ages of four and ten I read but moderately and with absolute catholicity. We had in our household the usual meaningless miscellany that accumulates if the parents are not specifically literary. Thus I read whatever lay behind the glassed-in shelves of two dreary-looking black-walnut bookcases. I devoured the standard "boys' books" scornfully discarded by my elder brother. I bored my way through at least ten volumes of an unreadable set of historical novels by some worthy named Mühlbach, I think, and got absolutely nothing from them; the same result would be achieved were I to read them now. I read an adventure story about the Belgian Congo that made an anti-imperialist out of me when I was eight; I have seen no reason to change my views since then. Something called *Buck Jones at Annapolis* similarly made me permanently skeptical of the warrior virtues.

I read an odd collection of "daring" books that many families of the period kept around the house, often hidden under lock and key: Reginald Wright Kaufman's *The House of Bondage;* something called *The Yoke,* which was on the same order; Maupassant complete, though this may not have been until I had reached the mature estate of twelve or thirteen; and similar luridnesses. These had no effect of any sort on me, as far I can recollect, though I suppose a psychoanalyst could, at a price, make me tell a different story.

The child reader is an automatic selecting mechanism. What he is not emotionally ready to absorb, his mental system quietly rejects. When in later years I became a teacher of literature I could never see the point in censoring my young charges' extracurricular reading. Very often the mothers (never the fathers) of my high-school students would ask me to explain my refusal to forbid Mary or John to read James Joyce's *Ulysses*. I never offered any satisfactory explanation except to say that if John or Mary were ready to understand *Ulysses* then they were ready to understand *Ulysses,* which was a Good Thing. If they were not ready to understand it, which was apt to be the case, then *Ulysses* would at most waste their time, on which I was not prepared to set any exaggerated value. Often an anxious mother would inquire whether I didn't agree that the last chapter (Mrs. Leopold Bloom's uncorseted memories of an exuberant life) was shocking. My reply may have been frivolous, but it seems to me it contained the germ of the truth: that she found it shocking mainly because she had not had the chance to read *Ulysses* when she was seventeen, wherein Mary or John had an advantage over her. This generally closed, without settling, the controversy.

As you can see, part of my four-to-ten reading was orthodox for a small child (I forgot to tell you that I also toddled through a volume of Ibsen, and found him impenetrable) but the unorthodoxies had no effect whatsoever. What I really liked was what any small boy or girl would like—what I was ready for. This included, of course, a moderate amount of what is called trash —the Rover Boys, Horatio Alger, Wild West yarns, Jack Harkaway, the whole conventional canon of those days.

I say trash. Actually such books are "trash" only by standards which should not be applied to children's reading. They have the incalculable value that listening to perfectly inane adult conversation holds for children: they increase the child's general awareness. They provide crude paradigms of character, motivation, life experiences. That is why it seems to me that the trash of my generation was superior to the trash of today. I submit that *The Rover Boys in the Everglades* and *Frank on a Gunboat* are preferable to Superman and his kind on two counts: they were cleanly and clearly written, and their characters were credible and not entirely unrelated to the child's experience. When I was nine I could learn something interesting about life from even such highly colored affairs as the Frank Merriwell series, but I know that my son can learn nothing whatsoever of genuine interest (that is, which he can check against the expanding universe within himself) from the comics. I believe firmly that the current juvenile literature of the impossible is meretricious compared with the honest hackwork my own generation enjoyed.

Between ten and seventeen I did the major bulk of my reading. I have never read as many books per year since, nor do I expect to in the future. Those were the splendid years, and it is my notion that they are the splendid years of most devoted readers. After seventeen (in some cases a year or two later) the books choose you, not you the books. You read within limits. Reading becomes a program. You read as part of your college curriculum, or to gain knowledge in a specific field, or to be able to bore your neighbor at dinner-table conversation.

Even the reading done during one's college years lacks the spontaneity, the high waywardness of one's pre-adolescent and adolescent reading. It circles around the classroom. It consists of authors recommended by authority or who you feel should be "covered." Or it has to do with books you know a good deal about in advance, one of the most effective ways to spoil one's reading pleasure. Such reading may be mentally stimulating or socially useful. It may benefit you in a dozen ways. But it is not an adventure in quite the same sense that reading in your second decade so often is.

I am not, in this random biblio-autobiography, proposing to list the books I have read. Nothing could be duller or less useful, except when he who does the listing owns a mind whose operations are really of interest to mankind, as was the case, for example, with John Stuart Mill. All I am here endeavoring to do is to out-line some of the processes whereby an average person became an about-the-average reader, which is what I immodestly claim to be. To understand these processes a mere catalogue of titles is of no avail.

Yet I would like to list a few names, mainly to indicate the kind of writer that, as I recall, influenced the more bookish boys and girls of my generation. Shaw, Galsworthy, Bennett, Conrad, Merrick, Barrie, Moore, Dunsany, Yeats, Synge, Swinnerton, Chesterton, Meredith, Wilde, Hewlett, Gissing, Zangwill, and above all H. G. Wells—these, to confine the list to Englishmen only, are a few of the authors I remember devouring from my tenth to my seventeenth year, miscomprehending many, over-prizing some, but getting from all an exultant sense of discovery, a peak-in-Darien thrill rarely enjoyed since.

The secret of second-decade reading, of course, is that you are not really finding out what Shaw thinks or Conrad feels, but what *you* think and *you* feel. Shaw and Conrad and the rest are but handy compasses to guide you through the fascinating jungle of your young self. When I read Wells' *Tono-Bungay* at fourteen or fifteen, I found myself saying in delight, "But that's just the way I feel!" When I now read Thomas Mann's *Joseph* story I find myself thinking how true it is to the experience of men in general. There is a difference in the quality of the emotion. The grown-up emotion may be larger and wiser (and probably more pompous), but the boyish one is unique just because it is so utterly, innocently self-centered.

During this adolescent period of my reading life I had a lucky break. My brother, five years my senior and a student at Columbia College, was at the time taking a conventional survey course that used a sound standard anthology known, I think, as *Century*

Readings in English Literature, edited by Cunliffe, Pyre, and Young. For some reason, possibly a mild fraternal sadism, he made me take the course along with him—he at college, I at home. The whole thing was over my head—I was fourteen—but when I had finished my *Century Readings,* which took a year, I had at least a hazy notion of the course and development, from *Beowolf* to Stevenson, of the most magnificent, after the Greek, of all literatures. I remember writing essays, perhaps no more interminable than my subjects, on Hakluyt and Spenser. I am still unable to dislodge from my memory—which is not a good one—odd lines of verse from minor poets like Drayton. That is all of no account. The important thing is that I got through my head at an early age a few simple truths: that the proper reading of a good writer requires energy and application; that reading is not mere "diversion"; that it is impossible to admire writing you do not understand; that understanding it does not destroy but rather enhances its beauty; that unless a writer's mind is superior to, more complicated than, your own, it is a bore to read him. (That is why I never recommend a book to a person if it is on his own mental level.)

I learned also that daydreaming and intelligent reading do not go together. There is a story told by Dr. Sandor Ferenczi, the psychoanalyst, about a Hungarian aristocrat who, while devouring a quick lunch between trains, was recognized by a boorish acquaintance.

"My dear Count! How are you?"

"Umph."

"And how is the Countess?"

"Dead."

"How shocking! It must be terrible for your daughter."

"She's dead."

"But your son—"

"Dead! Everybody's dead when I'm eating!"

During my all-out period everybody was dead when I was reading. Most children and adolescents know this magical secret of concentration, though it is not till they are older and duller that they realize it was magical.

I remember that, when I was fourteen, we lived about two miles from the nearest library. I had a choice. I could cycle there, borrow my books, and cycle back in a very few minutes—but those few minutes were lost to reading. Or, if I wished, I could walk to the library, reading the last fifty or seventy-five pages of my calculatedly unfinished book en route, make my borrowings, and walk back, reading a new volume on the way. I usually preferred the latter procedure. It is no trick at all to read while walking, to step off and onto curbs with unconscious skill, to avoid other pedestrians while your eyes are riveted to the page. There was a special pleasure in it: I had outwitted Father Time. I think Providence meant me to be an ambulant reader, for I never once even stumbled. But one afternoon when I was cycling home from the library with my wire basket full of books, I was hit from behind by a car and sent sprawling.

This absorption, this "losing yourself" in a book, though clearly quite remote from "practical life" (for children "practical life" is simply what grownups want them to do), is not daydreaming. The child does not interpose a continuous, fuzzy, wavering screen of personal desires and wishful visions between himself and the page. On the contrary, he and the page are one. The Victorian female, with whom novel reading was a disease, was the real daydreamer. For her, reading became a drug, a kind of literary marijuana, an instrumentality for the production of needed visions. The child's hearty relation to his book is devoid of this sick quality.

Well, the course my brother gave me, via that blessed trinity

Cunliffe, Pyre, and Young, was calculated to make me understand that literature, beyond helping one to discover oneself, has a higher, more impersonal function. It is a challenge issued by a higher mind, the author's, to a lower mind, the reader's. Even if the challenge is not met, much pleasure may still result. But if it is met, or if a sincere attempt to meet it is made, a finer, rarer pleasure is experienced. If you read for pure diversion, well and good, but if you read for any other purpose, always read above yourself. One of the reasons for the general mental fuzziness of most "cultivated" people we know is that publishers have become too shrewd. They have learned, the cunning little fellows, just how to temper their books to the lamblike mental innocence of their readers. The result is that every week we are deluged with books which, the publishers assure us, we can understand. It is quite true. We *can* understand them, all too easily. It would be much better for us if now and then we read a book just a few rungs beyond our mental capacities in their most relaxed state.

My second-decade reading—and I think this is sadly true of most of us—was in this sense educationally more valuable than any I have done since. During adolescence our feeling of bewilderment and insecurity tends to be greater than at any other time. Hence the need to know, to learn, is greater. Therefore whatever reading is done is intense. It is utterly assimilated. We pay absorbed attention to it, as we would to the instructions of an expert before venturing into a trackless forest.

It seems to me that in my late teens I did more "heavy" reading and digested it more thoroughly than at any succeeding period. In this connection I recall two antithetical experiments I made extending over an interval of six months. The first was an experiment in difficult reading. The other was an experiment in non-reading.

One summer I decided to spend my evenings reading only

"hard" books. I went at it with the humorless obstinacy of a six-teen-year-old—and I was more humorless and more obstinate than most. I staggered wildly through stuff like Ueberweg's *History of Philosophy,* Winwood Reade's *Martyrdom of Man,* Saintsbury's *History of English Prosody,* Taine's *History of English Literature,* Gibbon's *Decline and Fall of the Roman Empire.* It was enough for a book to seem important and for-bidding—I read it at once. No novels, no light literature of any sort, no magazines for three solid months—hot months, too. Now, as I look back on this extravagant experiment, it seems like the disagreeable behavior of a young prig. Yet I was not really priggish; I didn't read for show-off purposes. I read my Ueberweg as a challenge to myself, as a test, as a deliberate gesture, if you will, of self-punishment. The boy of sixteen by overexercise will punish his body deliberately just to see how much it can take. That same boy may punish his mind in the same way. It is a kind of initiation ceremony that he performs upon himself, a queer, grotesque test of approaching manhood. Sometimes he will decide to go right through the Encyclopaedia Britannica.

Well, that was Experiment Number One. The second was its opposite. I decided to spend three whole months reading nothing at all, not even a daily newspaper. (The three months coincided with a long absence from school, so the conditions for the ex-periment were at their optimum.) Now, why did I want to do this? It was again a matter of self-testing. I felt I had grown too dependent upon other people's ideas. The only way I could per-ceive to cure myself of this dependence was to abjure other people's ideas completely. The mental life of the adolescent is frequently characterized by this oscillatory quality. He can find out what his real nature is only by leaping from one extreme to the other.

And so for three months I read, as nearly as I can recall, virtually nothing. It was by no means a fruitless experiment, and to those held too tightly in the grip of the reading habit I heartily recommend it. The effect is purgative. The mind disgorges a good deal of waste and clutter, it slows down, for a time it seems vacant. Then gradually it fills again, this time not with the myriad, second-hand impressions induced by non-stop reading, but with the few clear ideas and desires that reflect more accurately your true self. The experience, in addition to being cleansing, is humbling; you realize how sparse is the net content of your mind.

I have known men and women who read so voraciously and continuously that they never have the time or opportunity to discover who they really are. Indeed, I suspect it is precisely because they prefer not to make that discovery that they cling so limpetlike to books. I suppose this is better for them than alcohol or hasheesh, but it is not very different. All of us, I am sure, have noticed people who suffer from reader's fidgets. If there is a book, a magazine, any piece of print within easy reach, they will at once take it up, idly, without real intent to peruse it, but out of a kind of mechanical compulsion. They will do this while they are talking to you, while you are talking to them, while engaged in some other activity. They are victims of print. Perhaps some dim premonition that unless I watched out I too would become afflicted with reader's fidgets made me carry through with entire success my three months' literary fast.

Some years ago I helped to manage a bookstore featuring a circulating library. The main body of customers consisted of commuters. Every evening, a few minutes after five, the commuters would dash in.

"Give me a novel!"

"Any special title?"

"No, any novel will do: it's for my wife"—as if that somehow made everything clear.

These commuters' wives—there are tens of thousands of them —were not really in any active sense doing any reading at all. They were taking their daily novel in a numbed or somnambulistic state. They were using books not for purposes of entertainment, but as an anodyne, a time-killer, a life-killer. Many "great readers" are of this class. Truth to tell, they have never read a book in their lives.

Akin to these novel-addicts are the newspaper fiends who read three, four, or five papers a day and supplement them with radio and TV news reports. There is only one Keeley cure I can recommend for this weakness, and that is for these people to save their papers for a week, and go back and read the news of seven days before. They will then see, even in the short perspective thus provided, how unimportant most "spot news" is. They will perceive that, if taken in over-frequent doses, its main effect is to bewilder or even to frighten, rather than to inform. A ration of one newspaper a day ought to be enough for anyone who still prefers to retain a little mental balance.

Serious reading is an art. An art is something you have to learn. To learn an art requires a teacher. There are too few such teachers of reading in the United States, and that is one of the reasons why we are still only a semi-educated people. I, like my fellow Americans, was never taught, in elementary and high school, how to read properly. Thus, when I reached college, I was but ill-equipped to understand any really original book that was handed to me, though I found no particular difficulty in getting through the required textbooks, manuals, and other predigested matter. I do not think I would ever have learned how to read had it not been for one man and one college course.

The man was John Erskine and the course was, rather absurdly, called Honors. Erskine himself was largely responsible for the conception underlying Honors, which in turn was the only begetter of Robert Hutchins' Chicago Plan, of the St. John's College classics curriculum, and in fact of the whole return in modern education to the great tradition of Western thought. John Erskine was a man of such varied talents that his original contribution to American education is often forgotten.

It is very hard to explain why Erskine was a great teacher. He was not a character as Copeland of Harvard was. Although always genial and fair, he never attempted to make the students like him. He did not act as if he were a perennial contestant in a popularity contest. (I am convinced, by the way, that those teachers who year after year are voted Most Popular by the undergraduates are rarely educators of great value.) In his literature courses Erskine never swooned over beauty or tried to make you "feel" the lines or the paragraph.

There were two things about Erskine that may help to explain the influence he wielded over his students, even over those who didn't care greatly about literature. One was his enormous respect (not merely liking) for his subject matter. This may seem a commonplace, but it is not. Many teachers—no more surprisingly than other frustrated human beings—have a silent, gnawing contempt for what they teach. Unaware of this contempt, they often find it subtly translated into a resentment of their students. The result is vitiated teaching, teaching of a purely formal sort.

Erskine not only loved his subject but reverenced it and respected himself for teaching it. There was thus a good moral relationship between himself and his work. It may seem highflown to say that this moral relationship was a vital aid in the production of good teaching. Yet I'm sure this was the case. He could teach his students to read because he had a large and lofty attitude toward what we were reading.

At the same time, if Erskine had been able to communicate only this attitude, he would not have been the great teacher he was. He went beyond this. To put it simply, he challenged us to *understand* what we were reading. He called upon us for a kind of mental exercise that is ordinarily devoted to mastering such "hard" subjects as philosophy and the sciences. (Actually, there are no "hard" or "easy" subjects. Donne is as difficult and as rewarding as Euclid.) Erskine made us work and the odd thing about it was that the more we understood, the more we liked the particular book we were reading.

The Honors Course was but a systematic extension of the Erskine educational program. For two years, under the guidance of a group of selected instructors, we read and talked about one great book a week, beginning with Homer and concluding, as I recollect, with William James. That was all there was to the course, and it was by far the most valuable one I took at college. You will find a good account of it and its influence in *How to Read a Book*. (Mortimer Adler was also one of my teachers, and a first-rate one, too.)

Well, Erskine and a few other teachers (particularly the poet Mark Van Doren) plus the two years I spent in the excellent company of fifty or sixty of the great writers of all time taught me, I hope and believe, how to read. I was lucky.